Using Journals With
Reluctant Writers

To Mom, Dad, and Torree,
who have given me my past, present, and future.
Thanks for the help.

Using Journals With Reluctant Writers

Building Portfolios for Middle and High School Students

Scott Abrams

CORWIN PRESS, INC.
A Sage Publications Company
Thousand Oaks, California

For information:

Corwin Press, Inc.
A Sage Publications Company
2455 Teller Road
Thousand Oaks, California 91320
E-mail: order@corwinpress.com

Sage Publications Ltd.
6 Bonhill Street
London EC2A 4PU
United Kingdom

Sage Publications India Pvt. Ltd.
M-32 Market
Greater Kailash I
New Delhi 110 048 India

Printed in the United States of America

Library of Congress Cataloging-in-Publication Data

Abrams, Scott.

Using journals with reluctant writers: Building portfolios for middle and high school students / by Scott Abrams.

p. cm.

Includes bibliographical references.

ISBN 0-7619-7611-6 (cloth: alk. paper)

ISBN 0-7619-7612-4 (pbk.: alk. paper)

1. Portfolios in education—United States. 2. English language—Composition and exercises—Study and teaching (Secondary)—United States. 3. Socially handicapped children—Education—United States. I. Title.

LB1029.P67 A37   2000

371.93—dc21   99-050876

This book is printed on acid-free paper.

00 01 02 03 04 05 06 7 6 5 4 3 2 1

Corwin Editorial Assistant:	Kylee Liegl
Production Editor:	Diana E. Axelsen
Editorial Assistant:	Cindy Bear
Typesetter/Designer:	Lynn Miyata
Cover Designer:	Tracy Miller

Contents

Acknowledgments

My thanks to the reviewers:

Nancy Guth
Stafford County Public Schools
Stafford, Virginia

Stuart Fischoff
California State University—Los Angeles
Los Angeles, California

Sheryl Milam
Russellville Middle School
Russellville, Kentucky

Rob Owens
Washburn Rural High School
Topeka, Kansas

Carol Miller
Mineral Ridge High School
Mineral Ridge, Ohio

Merle Burbridge
Ramona Elementary School
Hemet, California

Lise Hogan
Pease Middle School
San Antonio, Texas

About the Author

Scott Abrams is an Alternative Education Teacher at Marshall Alternative High School in Bend, Oregon, where he has been teaching for the past 2 years. He began his teaching career on the islands of Barbados and Dominica, teaching Basic Skills for the Peace Corps. He then spent most of the next 14 years teaching exceptional students at the secondary level. During this time, he also spent 3 years teaching special education as Adjunct Professor with the University of Nevada. His professional interests include educating emotionally disturbed, at-risk, and special education students. He received his BA from the University of Washington and his MA in Special Education from the University of Nevada.

CORWIN
PRESS

The Corwin Press logo—a raven striding across an open book—represents the happy union of courage and learning. We are a professional-level publisher of books and journals for K–12 educators, and we are committed to creating and providing resources that embody these qualities. Corwin's motto is "Success for All Learners."

Introduction

The word *education* comes from the Latin *educere* or "to lead out." The suggested journal topics in this book are designed to aid educators in leading out or drawing out reluctant writers. As E. B. White put it, "Every writer, by the way he uses the language, reveals something of his spirit, his habits, his capacities, his bias. This is inevitable as well as enjoyable. . . . No writer long remains incognito" (Strunk & White, 1979, p. 67). Journal writing can be a useful tool for helping students reveal themselves and improve their communication skills through writing.

The journal activities that follow were developed with and for "alternative education" students. These students are the teenagers who don't fit into traditional settings, such as the chronic non-attenders, students who have trouble with the law, girls who are pregnant, students with learning difficulties, youth who question every authority figure, students who have trouble with drugs, teenagers who are having difficulty growing into adults. In short, these activities apply to the students who are at risk of failure in our system of education. Or, perhaps more accurately, students who are at risk because our system has failed to meet their needs.

With proper use, these journal topics can help teachers meet certain critical needs of high-risk students. Journals can be used as a tool of self-discovery, as an avenue for improved interaction, and as a means of providing students with relevant writing opportunities. Two of the most important ways the journals can be used are (a) to open a private dialogue between student and teacher and (b) to improve the use of writing among students as a means of communication.

◆ Opening a Private Dialogue

The effective use of journal writing can be developed in large classroom environments, even ones that have rapid turnover rates. With 20 to 25 students in a classroom setting, there is no way the teacher can hope to interact daily with every student on a personal level. A private journal entry, with honest responses, can provide the basis for personal dialogue between teenager and adult, a condition not present in the lives of many students. I've found these practices to be most effective in developing such a relationship.

1. Always read the entries as soon as possible. Journals can be an extremely effective means of dialogue as long as students know you care enough to read their thoughts and reply daily.

2. Jot a personal note to the student whenever possible. This increases the possibility of dialogue and lets the student know you've read the entry. Try to refrain from judgments and give advice only when asked.

3. Never criticize or use a red pen. Journal entries are a means of expression, not a formal writing assignment. Their purpose is to encourage writing as communication; they were not designed as formal assessment tools. Red is often a stop sign for students.

4. Give the students an out (like putting a X at the top of the page) if they don't want you to read an entry. Make sure they know there are certain topics like suicide or abuse that you must report if you read an entry that tells about a specific incident.

5. Don't force the students to stick to a topic. The idea is to allow free-flowing written expression, not to follow a set of guidelines.

6. Whenever possible use current situations inside or outside the classroom for relevant journal topics.

7. Finally, remember that many students don't like to use writing as a means of expression, so encouragement and building trust are key components to a successful use of the journals.

The journal topics in this book are set up to correspond to a typical school year but can be used in any order. They begin with general nonrevealing, nonthreatening ideas. These topics will help to introduce writing as a means of expression and allow the student to test the teacher's reactions before encountering material that requires more personal responses. The topics have multiple questions because many students (especially reluctant writers) will answer any question with as few words or as simple a sentence as possible.

Each topic also includes a quotation that could be used as a prompt; a suggested video; an essay prompt (see the portfolio section); and an extension activity (to give students a different way to process their thinking). Related reading possibilities are included for half of the topics. The questions developed from the videos and reading material are not meant to be comprehensive but simply additional writing prompts to stimulate interest. Even though a short summary is included, teachers will need to preview all the videos (they are rated PG or PG-13) and the readings to see if they contain material that would be objectionable in their specific educational setting. Teachers are encouraged to use the material while at the same time reshaping it to fit their specific needs.

Improving the Writing Process ◆

There are three important ways these journal entries can improve the writing process for reluctant students. They supply an audience, increase motivation, and provide a foundation for further teaching.

The Audience

One of the keys to increasing a student's desire to communicate effectively in writing is to increase the importance of the audience. Many students who shut down completely when a term paper is required, will eagerly write a letter to a friend. The desire to spell and to use grammar correctly becomes important because the need to communicate effectively is much greater. If the teacher, through the use of journal dialogue, can become an important audience, the student will attempt to become a better writer and communicate more clearly.

Motivation

Almost everyone has a passion. For many students, that passion lingers beneath layers of apathy, anger, or confusion. Journal entries can help a teacher discover what motivates each student. Often there are only one or two topics that interest young writers, but those are the subjects that can prompt their best efforts. The native-Alaskan teenage mother who wrote pages about her baby (see Student Sample 1) wrote only a line or two on every other subject for the school year. The Hispanic teen who wrote a page about gangs (Student Sample 15) wrote virtually nothing the rest of the semester. Give students enough chances to explore their interests, and, somewhere along the line, you will hit upon an area that results in an effective essay. These are the efforts that can provide a basis for a writing portfolio response.

◆ A Foundation for Further Writing: Building a Portfolio

Perhaps the most important academic use of journals is that they can provide a basis for further writing. Just as a top-notch basketball player develops and hones his or her skills on the open court, unfettered by strict interpretation of rules, a creative writer can develop style and voice through the use of a journal. However, the best basketball players reach their potential only when playing within a team framework that includes coaching on basic fundamentals as well as on the finer points of the game. So, too, the young writer needs a structured forum in order to develop his or her writing skills fully.

The journal topics in this book are arranged in a way that gives teachers the opportunity to provide greater structure. Each topic is divided into four daily segments. A formal essay could be required once a week to incorporate the daily entries. For example, after writing for 4 days about schools in their journals, students could be required to expand their entry on the perfect school into an expository essay. The less formal journal entry becomes a rough draft, which gives the students the opportunity to rethink and rewrite their original copy. This process further aids in the development of young writers. Several different forms of writing can be developed from the journal topics, including expository, narrative, and persuasive essays, as well as poetry.

Expository Writing

An expository or explanatory essay, in its simplest form, consists of the following:

I. Definition (what is being explained)

II. A Sequenced Explanation
   A. Description of the Parts
   B. Operations (how and why it works)
   C. Applications (when and where it works)

III. Interesting Special Features

IV. Concluding Statements

Besides describing the perfect school, other subjects that lend themselves to expository writing are "Home," "Family," "Talents," "Sports," "Cliques and Gangs," and "Uniqueness." Using comparisons and contrasts is another way to facilitate students' attempts at expository essays. An example essay could be "Compare your family to your best friend's.

How are they different? How are they the same?" Having students take another point of view is another way to enhance creativity: "How would your mother describe your family?"

Two student samples of expository writing follow. The first was written by a teenage mother who wrote very little on any other subject for the rest of the year. The second was written by a high school sophomore who had a great deal of difficulty coming up with an essay topic of interest.

Student Sample 1

Having a baby has changed my whole life around, but it is worth it cause baby's are very special people and very special in our life. When they are first born they are mostly sleeping during the day. They also wake up in the middle of the night to be fed and to get their diaper changed. Then as days pass they begin staying awake longer, eating more and getting bigger. Baby's like to look around a lot, see all the different things and colors. They begin moving their arms and legs around. You have to wash the bottles and be sure they aren't sour. Check the milk to be sure it isn't sour and you need to give them a bath about two times a week. You have to make sure the house is warm and there is no cold air coming in. After three and a half months you can begin feeding them baby cereal. They begin holding up their head at about four months. Baby's start to crawl at about six months. Most baby's jump in a johnny jumper to make their legs strong or have a walker so they can learn to walk also to know what their legs are for. The baby needs to be warm so you need to make sure he or she is dressed the right way for the weather. The first six months about you need to boil the water. Also you need to be patient with the baby that is if they are spoiled (like our son.). Baby's go through a lot of milk and diapers. Every mother raises their baby different, but this is how I see Derek John. Baby's begin to walk when they are pretty close to one year old or some do after they are one, I think it depends on the mother. Baby's begin to do a lot of things like pull hair, pinch, sit up, stand up, hold their own bottle while drinking it and start wanting things. After baby was born I couldn't believe it so I stayed up all night just looking at him.

Student Sample 2

Black Sabbath is one of the greatest heavy metal bands ever. They are a legend in rock n' roll. They are the reason heavy metal is the way it is now. Black Sabbath started as Polka Tulk and changed their name to Earth in 1967. They became Black Sabbath in 1969. Many other bands look up to Black Sabbath and are sing-ing because of inspiration from Black Sabbath. They are so great that when the tickets for their Portland, Oregon, concert became available the local tickets were sold out in two weeks.

Ozzy Osbourne, whose real name is John Osbourne, does the vocals for Black Sabbath. He has some of the coolest songs like—"Ironman, "Electric Funeral," "Psycho Man," "War Pigs," "Sabbath Bloody Sabbath," "Black Sabbath," "Paranoid," "Crazy Train," "Good-bye to Romance," "I Just Want You," "Into the Void," etc. etc. All of these songs are great because they are sung by fabulous people, and the music is transcendent. The guitars, drums, and vocals are magnificent, and a lot of people can relate to the lyrics.

He also has some of the greatest lyrics from "Good-bye to Romance"—"Good-bye to all my friends, I guess that we'll meet, we'll meet in the end." These lyrics mean a lot to me be-cause my best friend and I don't see each other as much as we used to, but when we do we feel like we've been together forever and when we say good-bye we always know we will see each other again. Also from "I Just Want You"—"There are no unlockable doors, there are no unwinnable wars, there are no identical twins or forgivable sins." He is saying everyone is their own person and can do anything. And from "Sabbath Bloody Sabbath"—"Nobody will ever let you know, when you ask the reasons why. They'll just tell you that you're on your own, fill your head all full of lies." This song explains that people and au-thority don't tell you everything you want to or need to know and sometimes they lie about the truth and try to manipulate you.

Ozzy left Black Sabbath once in 1977 and again in 1978 and started Blizzard of OZZ and left them to go solo for 17 years. They decided to get back together for another great perfor-mance for their millions of screaming fans for the BLACK SABBATH REUNION TOUR.

Narrative Essay

The telling of stories, or narrative essays, is a natural outgrowth of the journal writing process. Broken into its simplest form, a narrative essay is composed of the following:

I. Orientation (who, when, where)

II. Events that lead to a problem (includes details for development)

III. Resolution of the Conflict

Students could write fanciful narratives for topics such as "Trading Places," "The Future," and "What Dreams May Come." Nonfiction narratives could be required for "Life Summary," "Being Alone," or "Coming of Age."

A short narrative example follows, written by a student who was arrested again shortly after he wrote these words:

Student Sample 3

I really wonder why I got caught smoking budds because I thought I would never get caught because I had been doing it for so long. Maybe it was meant for me to be caught because there are a lot of good reasons. I am going to go see my attorney today at 2:15 because I'm going to court next Thursday at 8:30. I'm probably going to receive probation time and be drug tested every now and then so it will keep me clean for that time. If they put me in some kind of good rehab program I'll probably stay clean forever but if they don't I'm looking forward to smoking once I'm off probation.

Persuasive Essays

Another type of writing that could be developed from the journal entries is the persuasive or argumentative essay. In its simplest form, the persuasive essay can be broken into the following:

    I. Introduction (which point of view you are taking)

    II. Arguments for Your Point of View

    III. Arguments Against Your Point
       (especially if you can refute them)

    IV. Conclusion (reiterating why your point of view
        is the correct one)

Examples of persuasive essays could be derived from the topics "Grades," "Money," "Crimes," and "Punishments." Some possible essay titles could be "Grades Really Don't Mean Anything," "Money Can't Buy Happiness," or "The Threat of Prison Really Doesn't Stop People From Committing Crimes."

A persuasive essay example follows:

Student Sample 4

Skateboarding should be allowed downtown. Many people believe all skateboarders run amok and destroy, hurt, or ruin things. I admit that sometimes skateboarders might damage things, but not intentionally.

Many skateboarders use their skateboards as means of transportation in order to get to work or even to go to school. Sometimes they may be forced to go through downtown. Allowing them to go through downtown would make it easier for them to get places.

Many times people who drive cars and walk even break laws, but they are not prohibited from downtown. I have witnessed on several occasions cars speeding through downtown. I have also seen people crossing streets when and where you are not supposed to.

Skateboarders are no guiltier of breaking laws than anyone else. Police officers are not consistent in the way they enforce skateboarding laws. While my friends and I skated through downtown we were stopped by a police officer. He told my friend Joe to give him his skateboard. Knowing the law Joe said that it was his first offense so he should only get a warning. The police officer said he didn't care.

Skateboarders have just as many rights as anyone else. They should be allowed to go wherever they want as long as they aren't breaking the law.

Other Forms of Writing

Several weekly topics ("Talents," "Emotions," "Dating") lend themselves to the introduction of poetry. Free verse is a preferred means of expression for many teenage writers (see Student Samples 8, 9, 10). Music lyrics can also be a powerful tool for encouraging creativity. Whatever means you use to develop your students' writing, assessment plays a crucial role in the creation of a satisfactory final product.

◆ Assessment

Assessment of student responses can vary greatly depending on your purpose for using a journal in class. Minimum requirements could include using complete sentences and requiring an answer to each question listed for a specific topic. If you wish to ensure dialogue, a simple check-plus system with personal notes from the teacher and extra credit for + responses can give the students feedback without requiring a great time commitment from the teacher. Plus responses need not be based on length but can be based upon honesty and self-revelation.

Student Samples 5 and 6 are examples of + responses to the time line prompt found in the "Life Summary" section. The first student was extremely intelligent but for the most part uninterested in school. Although he was flippant in his responses, they did show genuine thought. You can't force an honest or self-revealing response, but you can encourage thoughtful efforts. The second sample was written by a girl who had moved a great deal and therefore had missed out on completing high school credits. She never said much in class but really used the journal as a means to connect with the teacher in an extremely open manner.

Student Sample 5

1980 I was born
1986 Started school—hated it
1992 Was arrested for the first time
1996 Got kicked out of high school
1997 Hope to graduate
2001 Hope to get out of the country
2002 Move to Amsterdam
2007 Die but get reincarnated as a frog
2008 Get a commercial for Budweiser

Student Sample 6

1980 Born in California
1987 First crush and kiss
1988 Mother remarried
1992 Moved to Texas
1993 Moved to Nevada
1994 First real kiss—first boyfriend, ran away for two weeks
1995 Moved to Utah
1996 Began high school, made friends, learned to party,
      lost virginity
1997 Feb. learned to ditch class—summer met lots of people,
      hung out with friends, had lots of fun, learned a lot about
      people, how they act.
1998 Staying away from boys (only trouble) getting an education,
      hoping to graduate

Positive responses need not be lengthy. Student Sample 7 is a collection of student responses from the "Family" section of topics. Some of the responses were pulled out of longer entries, but they still reflect the level of honesty some students will reach when they feel comfortable with the reader of their journal.

Student Sample 7

. . . (my mother) she's not helpless or incompetent or anything but she seems slightly vulnerable . . .

. . . my step dad is okay—he's turned me in to the police a couple times but I know if I needed to talk to someone I could talk to him . . .

. . . every time I get in trouble, he's not there . . .

. . . he's been pretty good for my mom so I hope they stay together and don't let little things take them apart. He has six kids. My mom has four. So we have ten kids in the family not all of us live at home. But both of the fathers I have care about me just one doesn't take the time to show it . . .

. . . my dad is always hurting my feelings but when he gives me money he thinks he is making up for it . . .

I had to make a hard decision when my brother died. To me he was my life and without him I didn't want to be alive. To me I was like a clock that just stopped ticking and didn't ever want to tick again.

◆ Assessing Formal Writing

The second major function of assessment is to help students improve their writing ability. Although the purpose of the journal itself is to improve communication, each journal topic can be used in conjunction with formal writing prompts. These prompted essays can then be assessed and rewritten to enhance writing skills. A proficient writer uses his or her own "voice"; selects and develops a topic, using one or more main ideas with relevant supporting details; organizes the paper logically, moving smoothly from one idea to the next; varies beginnings and lengths of sentences; and uses correct spelling, grammar, and punctuation.

Voice

Because every journal entry encourages personal responses, students writing daily in their journals will develop their own style. More formal responses focusing on "voice" can be developed through poetry. If the teacher defines a poetry assignment in terms of the meaning that students put into their poem, "voice" can be isolated. Student Samples 8, 9, and 10 give a variety of free verse responses. Sample 8 was written by an intelligent but indifferent student. He ended up in jail during the week of his high school graduation. Sample 9 was written by a girl who rarely came to school. When she did attend, she would participate only in activities that interested her, like art and poetry. Sample 10 was written by an angry iconoclast who lived for his music and loved to write song lyrics. Music can also be used as a tool for developing voice. When students feel free to express themselves, they are most apt to write distinctly with their own style and voice.

Student Sample 8 (in response to the "Cliques and Gangs" questions)

There are skateboarders who tend to ride skateboards. There are jocks who play with balls. There are cheerleaders who play with pompoms. There are stoners who play with drug highs. There are mauds who are rewriting the disco era. There are preps who play with credit cards. There are pimps who play with diseases. There are players who deal with diseases. There are people who forget about labels and live life the best they can. Sometimes you have to take the tags off your shirts so they don't bother you.

Student Sample 9 (written in response to the "Being Alone" questions)

After the war it is so quiet, because it is I, that stands here alone
　　Where has everyone gone?
　　Am I here alone?
　　Please someone answer, for I am so frightened . . . frightened of the coldness . . . the darkness . . . the silence. The houses have been demolished from rocks up above, I think it was God, but . . . why has he been cruel to the innocent people? The people and animals have been killed. For the war was so long and uncivilized. Will I have nightmares? Will I forget it? Why did they fight? These are questions I have to answer myself, because my conscience is gone too. So I am alone . . . Alone in the cold, empty world.

Student Sample 10 (written in response to the "Friendship" questions)

There are friends and there are acquaintances
There are friend and there are families
There are losers and there are winners
There are people who live under pessimistic wraths of hate.
And there are optimistic people who live everyday as a gift.
And then theres us . . .
Rejects to society who live everyday under a world of restric-
　　tions, and problems
We all knew only to hate until we all met
Now were somethin'
We're punx forever.

Selecting and Developing a Topic

Selecting and developing a topic should be one of the strengths of a program using these journal ideas. Students should be assessed on their ability to stick to the point, stay focused, and show knowledge of their topics. Because many of the essay prompts come directly from the journal entries, students should have personal knowledge of the topic. The teacher can then direct students on staying focused and sticking to the point.

Organization

One way teachers can help with organization (having a clear beginning, middle, and end, with good transitions) is by teaching the types of essays discussed in the portfolio section. Two samples of rough drafts on parents follow. Sample 11 was written by a young man describing his stepfather. He simply answered each journal question on the topic of "fathers" without regard to any type of organization. A teacher's assessment comments could redirect his responses into a logical sequence with a topic sentence and a conclusion. Student Sample 12 (written in response to the journal questions on the subject of mothers) has a good flow and is easy to read but lacks any kind of substance. A teacher's comments could lead the student to give examples of why her mother is wonderful or ask for specific instances when she felt like throwing her mother down the stairs.

Student Sample 11

My step dad is tall and buff and has a fro. He works at Reno Disposal. He lives with me. He is stern like a mug and serious. Sometimes he is funny when he's in a good mood. He don't clean, cooks at BBQ's only. I make him happy by being good that's the nicest thing I could do or I could help him fix his car or just being with him makes me think hes happy. I sometimes don't get along most of the time its all good.

Student Sample 12

My mother is so wonderful, I love her to death. Yea, of course there are times when I don't get my way and I just feel like throwing her down some stairs. But, other than that she is one of my best friends. My mother and I always do stuff together except lately it has been hard because of her new job and me working, going to school, and night school also. It seems so weird that I can miss her so much and live in the same house.

Fluency and Word Choice

Word choice and fluency focus on the writer's precision, originality, variety of words and sentences, and creativity. Samples 13 and 14 are used to show the ways choice and fluency can be developed. In Sample 13, the student asks a powerful and compelling question: How did my mother die? As a journal entry, this was an extremely honest response to the "Mysteries" questions. As an essay, it shows a great many weaknesses. Besides the grammatical errors, it also shows a lack of ability to use language. Assessment could focus on better sentence structure. Student Sample 14 flows much more smoothly. It reads easily but the word choice is not creative or original. Upon rewriting, this student could be encouraged to pick more descriptive words.

Student Sample 13

A mystery in my life is when my mother died in 1990. To this day I really not sure how it happened. I think I not ever find out but in my mind I think she is a hole lot happy because she OD on drugs, but I am not sure if that is true or not. In my mind it will always be a mystery to me.

Student Sample 14

One thing in my life that has always been a mystery to me is why my mother married my step father. I know she loves him but I don't know how she fell in love with him. I mean I can understand falling for the wrong person because I do it all the time, but I can't find one attractive quality in him. He's 15 years older than her. When they got married she was very attractive. She could've had any one she wanted. There were three other men that wanted to marry her around that time. One was rich, one was fun and cute, and the other was rich and fun. She chose the one that was broke, didn't know how to keep a job, was ugly, fat, and he had no personality to make up for the things he didn't have. I don't think I'll ever understand.

Grammar

Finally, basic grammar is essential for getting ideas across in writing. Student Sample 15 was written by a young man who needed help grasping the basic rules of the English language. His journal response (the only entry all year that elicited more than one sentence from him) obviously had a great deal of personal meaning. The "voice" component was powerful but he needed to use basic punctuation and capitalization in order to get his ideas across to the reader.

Student Sample 15 (written in response to the "Cliques and Gangs" questions)

Well first my group there brown people some are big some are small and speak spanish and some are mean and some are nice there are pretty girls to and then theres another group in brown they are gangs you don't want to mess with them and especially now I mean some gangs are carrying guns now just so they can make there gang grow big and put other gangs down just by kill-ing one and another they dress with baggy pants called dickies or ben davies same with shirts but one thing I hate is when your walking alone they stop and pick on ya they tell you que barrio or what set you claim it means what gang you frome but if your not walking alone they won't do nothing they would just stare at you or one of them is just walking alone he won't do nothing just walk by but when he's with his friends there all ackeding bad then he talks shit but in my case lucky I have some really good friends to back me up to help with a proplem but then I try not to hang around with them to much cause who knows what might happen with me and them peace

Using journals as daily practice and requiring weekly formal essays can provide students with the tools they need to become proficient writers. Each journal topic is followed by a video; half of the topics have related readings that can be used for a more comprehensive English course. However, all of the ideas in this book are simply starting points for teachers to develop and use in the manner that best fits their students and classroom environment.

School

I am always ready to learn, although I do not always like being taught.
—Winston Churchill (Peter, 1977, p. 297)

This week's topics center around school, what works and what doesn't work for students, who, like Churchill, may not fit into traditional settings or teaching styles.

+ Think back to elementary school. What is the first thing you can remember from elementary school? Was it good or bad? What else can you remember from your first years in school? What would you change about them if you could?

+ What is your favorite school subject? What do you enjoy most about school? What are you trying to get out of school? (A good time? A chance to see your friends? Something else?)

+ Think back on all your years in school. What teacher or teachers helped you the most? Describe them. Describe what they did that helped you. Were they strict, humorous, or easygoing? What are two things teachers can do right now to help you?

+ Describe the perfect school for you. What would the classes be like? Where would the school be located? What kinds of things would you study? How many students would there be at your school? Who would teach you? Would you have a principal or some other authority figure? Would you have a diploma to show that you graduated or some other form of recognition? How important is it for you to be recognized by others for your accomplishments?

◆ Essay Prompt

(Expository) Describe the perfect school for you. Use your journal entries as a rough draft to come up with a final essay.

◆ Extension Activity

Try to make a change in your school or classroom that would help you become a better student.

◆ Video

Dead Poets Society (Haft, Witt, Thomas, & Weir, 1989) stars Robin Williams as an eccentric teacher who encourages students at a staid prep school to be free thinkers, then gets blamed when they actually do think for themselves. The movie explores themes much wider than the school setting, including parental relationships, peer interactions, and coming of age.

- ◆ Have you ever had a teacher who used comedy as a way of interacting with students?

- ◆ Have you ever had a teacher who made fun of the students? How did that make you feel?

- ◆ How would you feel if you were Neal's parents? How would you react if you were their child?

- ◆ Write a different ending to the story. What if Neal hadn't committed suicide?

- ◆ Why is the ability to think for yourself so dangerous to traditional establishments like schools and governments?

- ◆ In what ways do you conform (at school, with your friends)?

- ◆ Have you ever had teachers who tried to teach you to think for yourself? How did they do that?

- ◆ Are there times when you pretend to be something that you are not?

Trading Places

2

Each man's work is always a portrait of himself.
—Samuel Butler (Bartlett, 1968, p. 756)

Students often dream about who they would like to be or what they would like to be doing. By writing about who they are not, perhaps they can see more clearly who they are.

- If you could trade your life for the life of any famous person, whom would you choose? Why? What are three ways you think that person's life is better than yours is?

- If you could live in any time of world history, when would you choose? How would it be different from this time? Why would it be better for you?

- If you could become any fictional character, what character would you choose and why? What power or talents does that character have that you don't? How would you use those talents?

- What are three things you would change about your life if you could? What prevents you from making these changes?

Essay Prompt

(Narrative) Write a story about an impending tragedy at a school (in the past or future) when your fictional superhero saves the day.

◆ Extension Activity

Draw a cartoon character that represents all the super powers you wish you had.

◆ Video

Ladyhawke (Shuler & Donner, 1985) is the story of a beautiful maiden and a handsome knight who have been cursed by an evil bishop. The woman becomes a hawk during the day and the knight becomes a wolf at night, while each continues to care for the other. Matthew Broderick plays an impish rogue who helps defeat the bishop and bring the couple back together. Set in a magical time with plenty of action, it is a story that keeps interest levels high.

- ◆ What do you know about the bishop when he says, "I believe in miracles. It's my job"?

- ◆ What would a nickname like "the Mouse" tell you about a person? When do his mouselike qualities come in handy?

- ◆ Is it easier for you to believe in fantasy, magic, or witchcraft in a story set a long time ago? Why?

- ◆ How do you react when you are afraid?

- ◆ Have you ever been on a quest?

- ◆ The priest seeks redemption. What is redemption? What did he do wrong?

- ◆ Have you ever sought redemption for something you did wrong?

- ◆ What human qualities do the wolf and the hawk demonstrate?

- ◆ What did the riddle "night without a day, day without a night" mean?

- ◆ Gaston doesn't exactly tell the truth when relating stories of Isabeau to Navarre. Is it all right to lie to help someone else?

- ◆ Do you consider this story to be one that ends happily ever after?

- ◆ Are there any real-life stories that end happily ever after? Can you imagine your own life ending happily ever after?

- ◆ What do you think will happen to Gaston?

Life Summary

3

Life is a tragedy for those who feel and a comedy for those who think.
—Jean de La Bruyere (Henry, 1945, p. 154)

Students are encouraged to reveal more of themselves by describing their life and their important experiences.

♦ Write your life story in 10 minutes.

♦ Create a time line of events in your life. What have been the three most important events in your life? Why are they important to you?

♦ How old were you when you made the biggest changes as a person? What kind of changes did you make, and why did you make them?

♦ Continue your time line into the future. What events would you like to celebrate when you are 70? What would you like to accomplish? What can you do now to start working on those goals?

Essay Prompt ♦

(Narrative) Write an account of the time in your life when you will make the greatest changes.

◆ Extension Activity

Make a collage of pictures or drawings that depict different aspects of your life.

◆ Video

Forrest Gump (Finerman, Tisch, Starkey, & Zemeckis, 1994) is a fanciful tale of an "idiot" who by fate or circumstance participates in many of the events that have shaped the past 40 years of U.S. history. Besides being a historical vehicle, *Forrest Gump* covers a spectrum of human events, including cancer, AIDS, and the trauma of Vietnam. Many students have already watched the movie, so be sure to give them a variety of prompts, such as looking at characters other than Forrest. Several scenes may not be appropriate for all educational settings, so be sure to preview before showing.

- What are some unusual things you remember from your preschool years?
- Do you believe in miracles? If so, what are some? If not, why not?
- Have you ever had a friend who followed you around that you didn't really want around and you couldn't get rid of?
- What's your most embarrassing moment?
- Would you want to meet the president? If you could ask him two questions or tell him two things, what would you say?
- Do you work for your family? What kinds of things do you do for them?
- What is the loneliest time you can remember?
- Have you ever told someone you loved him or her?
- Do you have family expectations to live up to (like Lt. Dan)?
- If Forrest Gump had to write his life story in 10 minutes, what would he write?
- What's the greatest loss you've ever suffered?
- What's the biggest surprise you've ever had?
- Would you say Forrest was gifted or an idiot?

Related Reading ◆

Maya Angelou's *I Know Why the Caged Bird Sings* (1969) is a beautifully written, powerful story of her life growing up in the South 60 years ago. Frank talk about her rape as an 8-year-old and her growth into womanhood (Chapter 35) may make certain sections inappropriate for some audiences. However, the chapters are written so that it would be easy to pull out specific stories to use in the classroom. In some ways the book is aimed at a female audience, but the prose is such that any young writer could learn from this masterful storyteller.

- ◆ Have you ever wished you could be another race?

- ◆ What is the most uncomfortable situation you have ever faced?

- ◆ Compare your hometown to Maya's.

- ◆ If you could rename your hometown, what would it be?

- ◆ If you wrote about your childhood, would you write mainly about the good experiences or the bad experiences? Which would be more interesting?

- ◆ Do you feel like everyone knows you in your hometown? How about in your school or your neighborhood?

- ◆ Maya says that excitement is a drug. What do you think?

- ◆ Where do you go to get away from the world?

- ◆ Do your weekdays revolve on a sameness wheel?

- ◆ Have you ever camped out in your backyard? Would you want to?

- ◆ How does someone become a good writer?

- ◆ Do you think it helps someone's writing if they read a lot?

- ◆ Does it help a writer to have a lot of experiences?

- ◆ Have you ever been to a funeral?

- ◆ How do teachers show they respect you?

- ◆ How does Ms. Kirwin treat Maya?

- ◆ How does Maya respond to her father?

- ◆ Does your home seem different after you've been gone for a long time?

Friendship

4

Friendship is almost always the union of a part of one mind with a part of another, people are friends in spots.
—George Santayana (Johnson, 1972, p. 48)

These questions about friendship allow students to examine who they are by taking a close-up view of their friends.

- Do you have a lot of good friends, or many acquaintances and just a few good friends? Are most of your friends older or younger than you? Do you have many adult friends?

- Describe your best friend. In what ways is your best friend similar to you? How is your friend different? Why would you say this person is your best friend?

- Do you have an easy time making friends? Do you have many friends of the opposite sex? Is it easy for you to be friends only with someone of the opposite sex? Why or why not?

- What are three things someone could tell about you by looking at your friends?

Essay Prompt

(Expository) Compare your friends with your family members. How are they the same? How are they different? What do you look for in your friends that you don't get from your family?

Extension Activity

Sit down at lunch (or some other free time) next to someone you don't consider a friend. See how the person reacts and how you feel talking to this person.

Video ◆

The movie *Breaking Away* (Yates, 1979) tells the story of four high school buddies in Indiana and how they react to the changes that inevitably come after graduation. It also tells of growing into adulthood and what it means to come from a lower socioeconomic class. The film could also be used for "Sports" (much of the story revolves around Dave's love of bicycling) or "Family" (Dave's father and his relationship with Dave are also important).

- Do you have favorite hangouts where you meet with your friends? Favorite places to go during the summer?
- Do you have a passion or a love that takes up all of your spare time?
- Do you enjoy swimming? Are you afraid to go in the water? How about really deep water?
- What would you think of a guy with the nickname "Moocher"?
- Is getting out of school a frightening experience?
- What things could you do (or have you done) to shock your parents?
- Have you ever pretended to be someone you weren't in order to get someone to like you? Did you have to tell the person you weren't really like that?
- Would you want to go to college if your best friends weren't going?

- Do you work during the summer or just hang out?

- Have you ever walked out on a job?

- Have you ever sent flowers or gone out on a limb to show someone you cared about them? How did you feel afterward?

- How do your parents try to get you to do what they want you to do? Do they try to talk to you or do they leave you alone to make your own decisions?

- What does "cutter" stand for? Why was it a derogatory term?

- How do you react when you are frustrated in reaching your goals?

- Have you ever felt ashamed of your friends?

- Do you take pride in your work?

- Do you like to compete against other people? How about yourself?

◆ Related Reading

Sharon Creech's (1994) *Walk Two Moons* (1995 Newbery Award winner) is a simply told but dynamic story about a young girl trying to find her way in life without her mother. Sal tells the story of her best friend Phoebe to her grandparents as they travel across the country to discover what has happened to Sal's mother. A painful but surprising ending makes this an especially powerful book.

- Do most of your friends have backgrounds (stories) similar to yours?

- What's the longest road trip you've made?

- If you had a name that was more descriptive of you (like an Indian name), what would it be?

- Did you ever invent stories with your friends about strangers that you meet or see around town?

- Why doesn't Sal send postcards?

- What do your parents think of your friends?

- Do you ever scare your friends? Do you like to watch horror movies with them?

- ♦ Have you ever gotten really tired of your friends and wished they would leave you alone but they don't? How do you deal with that? Do they get tired of you?

- ♦ Do you think your mother would like to walk out on your family?

- ♦ How do Sal's feelings about death change?

Family

5

> *Big sisters are the crab grass in the lawn of life.*
> —Charles Schultz (Princeton Language
> Institute, 1993, p. 169)

Students are encouraged to describe their family. By dissecting the different members of their family, students get the chance to see where they come from.

♦ Describe your mother. Is she tall, short, pretty, plain, light haired, dark haired? Does she work outside your home? What does she do on a typical day? What does she like to do on her days off? Does she like to cook? What does she like to eat? Does she watch much television? What do you think your mother wants most out of life? What is the best thing you could do for your mother?

♦ Describe the most important adult male in your life. Is he tall, short, handsome, ordinary, light haired, dark haired? Does he work outside the home? What does he do in his free time? Does he like to cook? What does he like to eat? Does he watch much television? What do you think he wants most out of life? What is the best thing you could do for him?

♦ Describe your brothers or sisters or stepbrothers or stepsisters. (If you don't have any, tell why you think your parents stopped after one child or how you think your life would be different with brothers and sisters.) Do you enjoy spending time with them?

What do they do that irritates you the most? Do they ever do nice things for you? What is the best thing you could do for them?

◆ Think of the last time your entire family was together (or a time when everyone was together that you remember especially well). Describe where it was and what happened. Was it a good time or a bad time? What could you have done to make it better? Do you wish you family would spend more time together? What activity would you want to do with your entire family?

Essay Prompt ◆

(Expository: Point of View) Describe your family from your mother's point of view.

Extension Activity ◆

Do three chores or family duties that you normally wouldn't do, and see how your family reacts.

Video ◆

Parenthood (Grazer & Howard, 1989) is a movie starring Steve Martin that goes in depth into the lives of Martin's family as well as his brothers and sisters. There are a variety of family types that should connect with most students. Some comedic and sentimental moments make the movie worthwhile; however, there are a number of sexual references, so teachers should be sure to preview before showing it in the classroom.

◆ Do your parents try to treat you differently than they were treated? Do they succeed?

◆ Which family in the movie is most like yours? Why?

◆ Have you ever had a grandparent or other family member come to stay with you?

◆ Do you respect your parents? Why or why not?

◆ Do you think people should have to have licenses to have children? What would the requirements be?

◆ Do your parents bail you out or let you suffer the consequences of your actions?

◆ What would you do for your children?

Home

6

We search the world to find the beautiful, yet unless it is within us, we find it not.

—Ralph Waldo Emerson (Peter, 1977, p. 65)

Students are encouraged to describe their world, starting with their bedroom and moving outward.

- ◆ Describe your bedroom. Is it big or small? What have you put on your walls? Do you have a lot of clothes? Do you have a clock? Television? Stereo? Is your bedroom clean or messy? What could someone tell about you by going into your bedroom?

- ◆ Describe the street where you live. Are people friendly to each other? Do you know much about your neighbors? What do the houses or apartments look like? What kinds of cars do people have? Are the buildings and lawns taken care of?

- ◆ Have you lived all your life in the same place? Where was your favorite place to live? What are two things you would change about where you live now?

- ◆ If you could live anywhere you wanted, where would you live? Why? Are you going to try to move there when you can make that choice? Why or why not?

Essay Prompt

(Expository) Compare your bedroom to your classroom at school.

Extension Activity

Keep your room cleaned up for a week. How did you feel with a clean room? How did your parents feel?

Video and Related Reading ◆

The movie *What's Eating Gilbert Grape* (Teper, Ohlsson, Matalon, & Hallstrom, 1994) describes a young adult's travails in a small town as he takes care of his 400-pound mother and his siblings after his father's suicide. Leonardo DiCaprio masterfully plays Gilbert's retarded brother who is always getting into trouble. The movie as well as the book by Peter Hedges (1991) are examples of family life and perseverance that can easily be used as comparison pieces. The book has two sexual scenes that may not be appropriate in some settings. The movie should also be previewed before showing.

- ◆ Compare your hometown to Gilbert's. How are they similar? How are they different?

- ◆ Do you ever go back to visit your former teachers?

- ◆ Who takes care of most of the responsibilities in your family?

- ◆ Are there areas of your hometown that are dying out because other areas are becoming more popular?

- ◆ Do you know anyone who just hangs out and watches television all the time?

- ◆ Why does Gilbert take care of his family instead of just taking off?

- ◆ Would you stay at home and take care of your family (like Gilbert), or would you take care of your own needs?

- ◆ Are you proud of your house or family? Are you ashamed?

- ◆ Why has Gilbert's mother given up on life?

♦ Would you want to burn your house down? Why did Gilbert burn his?

♦ What will happen to Gilbert's family without his mother? Will he stay with Arnie? What will become of the sisters?

♦ What will happen to the small town where Gilbert lives?

Talents

7

Genius is 1% inspiration and 99% perspiration.
—Thomas A. Edison (Henry, 1945, p. 104)

These questions give students the opportunity to discuss their favorite kinds of music and to examine their own artistic abilities.

- Who are your favorite singers or music groups? What is it about them that you like? Do you like the music? The lyrics? The music videos? What are your favorite song lyrics? What is it about them that you like?

- What is your least favorite kind of music? Why? Do you like music from other eras? Country music? Classical music? Oldies? Do your parents like your music? Why or why not? Do you think you will like your children's music?

- They say music is the universal language. Almost everyone likes some kind of music. Do you think that's true? Why do you think most people like music? Do your friends like the same music as you?

- What are two talents or abilities you have? What are two talents or abilities you would like to have? Could you work to get them? Why or why not?

◆ Essay Prompt

(Poetry) Give students an opportunity to use free verse to express themselves, such as writing a poem about their favorite musical group or creating their own song lyrics. If students have trouble getting started, have them read a poem like "The Cremation of Sam McGee" (Service, 1940). Start them off with the first half of each line of the poem and let them create the rest using their own characters and settings.

◆ Extension Activity

Listen to three classical songs. What did you think about as you listened to them?

◆ Video

Mr. Holland's Opus (Cort, Nolin, Field, & Herek, 1995) examines an influential teacher's career. More than just a celebration of the arts, the movie goes into issues such as family responsibilities, careers, and personal self-worth.

- ◆ Have you ever taken a music appreciation course? Would you like to?

- ◆ Have you ever had a teacher who used modern music to teach you? Would you like to have one who did?

- ◆ How does Mr. Holland show his students that he cares about them?

- ◆ Why is his son's deafness so hard to handle?

- ◆ Have you ever thanked one of your former teachers?

- ◆ How did Mr. Holland grow as a teacher? As a father?

- ◆ Have you ever taken music lessons or lessons to learn some other kind of skill? If not, would you like to? If so, how did you feel when you first started?

- ◆ How important are art and music classes in high school? Compare them to academics. How about sports?

- ◆ How did Mr. Holland feel about his opus?

- What is the most creative thing you have ever attempted?

- When you retire, how do you want to measure your success?

- How important is it for you to make lots of money?

- How important is it for you to be creative?

- How important is it for you to help people?

- How important is it for you to have a family?

Fears

8

Keep your fears to yourself, but share your courage with others.
—Robert Louis Stevenson (Safir & Safire, 1982, p. 125)

Beginning with Halloween, students are invited to look at their fears and how fears affect their lives.

- What did you do for Halloween this year? What other Halloweens do you remember? What was your favorite Halloween?

- Do you like horror movies? How do they make you feel? What is your favorite? Why do you like it?

- Are you afraid of certain animals? Snakes? Spiders? Why do you think so many people are afraid of snakes and spiders in our society? Is fear learned, or is it a survival mechanism from when we had reason to fear certain animals?

- What is the most frightened you've ever been? Do you enjoy being frightened? Do you enjoy the adrenaline rush of a new experience? Do you ever go out and seek those new experiences?

◆ Essay Prompt

(Narrative) Write about your most frightening experience (fact or fiction). Set the scene and try to make the reader experience your fear.

Extension Activity

Find a picture of something that frightens you or try something that frightens you, like giving a speech in front of a large audience. Objectively record how you feel.

Video

The River Wild (Foster, Truman, & Hanson, 1994) stars Meryl Streep as an outdoorsy adventure seeker who decides to take her son on a raft trip. Her mousy, architect husband comes along as well as a couple of robbers who turn the trip into a survival struggle. If the movie is screened ahead of time the one "F..." by Terry as they finish "the gauntlet" can easily be avoided (by fast forwarding). The film could also be used for "Family," "Occupations" (outdoors vs. indoors), "Experiences," and "Leaders."

- ◆ Have you ever gone on a trip with your parents but without your brothers or sisters? Would you like to?

- ◆ Have you met anyone who seemed fun at first but turned out to be a real jerk? How did you react to that person?

- ◆ What are the first indications that Wade and Terry aren't what they seem?

- ◆ Does adversity help bring people together?

- ◆ Have you ever gone through a difficult situation and become closer to the people you were with?

- ◆ What are 10 uses for a Swiss army knife?

- ◆ What are five essentials for traveling in the outdoors?

- ◆ How does knowing sign language help Gail's family?

- ◆ Do you know any parents whose work seems more important than their family?

- ◆ Have you ever been drifting along through life, just letting the current take you where it wants?

- ◆ Could you shoot someone if it meant saving your family?

- ◆ Would Terry have been a criminal if he had chosen better friends?

- ◆ How do you think Gail's family will change after their experience?

◆ Related Reading

Touching the Void by Joe Simpson (1988) describes his experience while climbing in South America. He breaks his leg, and his partner attempts to lower him thousands of feet down the steep face of a mountain. At one point they slip, Joe slides over a drop, and his partner has to cut Joe loose or they will both die. Joe ends up inside a crevasse, with no one to help, then spends 3 days crawling to safety. It's a gripping suspense story for older students interested in true-life adventure.

♦ Would you like to travel to another country? Why or why not?

♦ Would you like to climb a mountain?

♦ Why do people climb mountains?

♦ If you wanted to climb a mountain, would you take the easiest way up, or would you want to try a way that no one else had climbed even if it was very dangerous?

♦ Your best friend is hanging from a rope with you on the other end. If you cut the rope, your friend dies. If you don't cut the rope, both of you will die. What do you do? How would you feel? What would you tell his or her family and friends?

♦ If a good friend of yours died climbing with you, would you keep climbing? Why or why not?

♦ If you almost died doing the sport you loved, would you keep trying it?

♦ What's the longest you've gone without eating?

♦ Have you ever felt like you were going to die? What happened?

♦ What parts of Joe Simpson's survival epic were luck, and what parts of his survival were dependent upon his skill?

♦ Who do you think would be more likely to climb again, Joe or his partner?

Sports

9

Winning isn't everything, it's the only thing.
—Vince Lombardi (Peter, 1977, p. 11)

Sports is a topic of interest to many teenagers, and with these journal entries students have the opportunity to explore their personalities through the meaning they place on competition.

+ Do you enjoy physical activities? Do you like P.E. at school? Why or why not? Why do they make you dress especially for P.E. when so many students don't like to?

+ Do you like to watch sports? Which ones are your favorites? What are your favorite sports teams? Do you usually root for a team or for specific players?

+ Would you rather play an individual sport or a team sport? Why? Would you rather be the best player on a mediocre team or just an average player on a championship team? How important is winning to you when you play on a team?

+ Would you rather compete against someone who is just as good or better than you are or someone who is almost as good but not quite as good as you are? How important is winning to you when you play for yourself? Are you a good winner? Are you a good loser?

◆ Essay Prompt

(Expository) Explain how to play your favorite sport.

◆ Extension Activity

Try inventing a game or activity that requires skills that most of the athletes in your classroom don't have. Give everyone a chance to play and experience different roles.

◆ Video

Rudy (Fied, Woods, & Anspaugh, 1993) is a true story about a Notre Dame football fan who never gives up on his dream to play for the Fighting Irish. He is too small, doesn't have good enough grades, and comes from a poor working-class family, yet he never gives up. The movie makes no false pretenses, and he plays only one or two downs, but there is still a pervading sense of triumph. This film could also easily be used in the "Family," "Dreaming," or "Being Alone" sections.

- ◆ How you ever been told you were too small, too slow, or too young to accomplish something? How did you react?

- ◆ "Dreams are what makes life tolerable." Do you agree?

- ◆ Do you still interact with your siblings the way you did 5 years ago?

- ◆ Is it a teacher's or counselor's job to encourage you to dream (even if your dreams are unreasonable) or to tell you what they believe are your best chances for success?

- ◆ How does the accident involving Peter change Rudy's life?

- ◆ Are you willing to take a long time to work hard and reach your goals, or do you want immediate satisfaction?

- ◆ How do you deal with disappointment and rejection?

- ◆ How do your parents react when they are proud of you?

- ◆ Have you ever quit at something important to you? How did you feel?

Expectations 10

The only place where success comes before work is in the dictionary.
—Vidal Sassoon (Princeton Language
Institute, 1993, p. 470)

By the 10th week of school most students are running into report cards, grades, and expectations. These topics allow students to examine their own work habits and expectations for success.

♦ What do grades mean to you? Does it matter to you what grade you receive? Do your parents provide incentives (money, privileges) to encourage good grades, or do your parents just expect you to get good grades?

♦ Do you ever rate your own work? Does it matter to you what other people think of your work? Are some people's opinions more important than others'? Whose opinions do you value the most?

♦ Would you rather work for someone who is always encouraging or someone who is sometimes critical and sometimes encouraging? Have you worked with people who are always critical? Do you feel encouraged at school to do your best? How could your school reward you more meaningfully?

♦ If you were to write a book or a song, would you rather get it published just the way you wrote it and have the book be unsuccessful, or would you rather have someone take your idea and make major changes but have the book be very successful? Do you ever write just for yourself or do you always write for others?

◆ Essay Prompt

(Persuasive) Agree or disagree with the statement: Grades don't really mean anything outside of school.

◆ Extension Activity

Try working especially hard in school for an entire week and see how people react to you.

◆ Video

Stand and Deliver (Musca & Menendez, 1987) gives the true-life account of Jaime Escalante, whose high standards and expectations turned around the math department at an inner-city school. The students start out as low achievers and end up passing the precollege entrance exam for calculus. The movie says a great deal about esteem and expectations and how teachers can turn students' lives around.

- Why do you think most teachers become teachers?
- Why do you think most students go to school?
- What do you want out of school?
- Have you ever tried to help someone who didn't want your help?
- How can teachers show you that they care? How do they show you they don't care?
- How would you raise test scores if you ran your school?
- Do students rise to the level of expectations? How do teachers and parents show you their expectations?
- Are boys afraid of "smart" girls?
- Why does the tester think Jaime's students have cheated? How would you feel if you were one of those students?
- Do you think most school officials trust their students?
- Can doing well in school help you in the other parts of your life?

Autumn Holidays

Men love war because it allows them to look serious. Because it is the one thing that stops women from laughing at them.

—John Fowles (Princeton Language Institute, 1993, p. 461)

Veteran's Day and Thanksgiving are used to start students thinking and writing about their country, ideals, and why they might be lucky to live in this country.

* Do you know anyone who has been in the military? Were they ever in combat? Do they talk about their experiences? How did being in the military change them?

* Are there certain people, things, or ideas that are important enough to you that you would give up your life for them? What if someone broke into your house and threatened you or your family? Would you risk your life to stop them? What if the robbers just wanted money?

* What do you remember most about Thanksgiving? What is your typical Thanksgiving like at home? Is there a special Thanksgiving you remember?

* Write about three things for which you are thankful.

◆ Essay Prompt

(Persuasive) Agree or disagree with the statement, "Freedom is worth dying for."

◆ Extension Activity

Give up part of your Thanksgiving for someone else (who is not related to you) this year.

◆ Video

In *The War* (Avnet & Turner, 1994), Kevin Costner plays a Vietnam vet who has returned to a shattered existence back home. The real story is that of his children and their battle with the Lipnickies (the local bullies). Through the war over their tree fort and its aftermath, the children learn the horrors of battle and the redeeming value of friendship.

- ◆ Have you ever built a tree fort?
- ◆ Do you have any friends from ethnic groups different than your own? Have you ever offended them without meaning to?
- ◆ How does it feel to get back together with someone you haven't seen for a long time?
- ◆ Have you ever known anyone who has spent time in a hospital because of mental problems?
- ◆ Have you ever dared someone? Did they follow through? Has anyone ever dared you to do something? Did you follow through?
- ◆ Have you ever gone on a scavenger hunt? Try making a list of things that would be hard but not impossible to find.
- ◆ Are you proud of your scars?
- ◆ How has the war affected Stephen's family?
- ◆ Have you ever had to go to summer school?
- ◆ What are three instances of prejudice in this story?
- ◆ Have you ever written your memoirs?
- ◆ Do you know anyone you would call a hero?

◆ Are there any families like the Lipnickies in your hometown?

◆ What's the greatest loss you've ever suffered? How did it change you?

Related Reading

Born on the Fourth of July describes Ron Kovic's (1976) disillusionment with the United States and its involvement in Vietnam. Three fourths of his body was paralyzed by gunfire. The book contains graphic scenes and speech, but Chapters 6 and 7 give a starkly compelling picture of the true horror of war.

◆ What kinds of choices did Kovic have as he lay in the hospital?

◆ What choices had he lost after becoming paralyzed?

◆ Do you consider yourself an independent person or someone who relies on others?

◆ How would you cope if you were forced to rely on others for activities as simple as eating, drinking, or getting dressed?

◆ What is a Communist?

◆ What countries were (or are) Communist? Why did the United States want so badly to stop Communism?

◆ Kovic describes a typical childhood of the 1950s. How would you describe a typical childhood of the 1990s?

◆ Would you say your childhood was typical?

◆ Do you think you would appreciate life more or less if you were almost killed but ended up paralyzed?

◆ Have you ever publicly protested anything?

◆ What causes would be worth protesting?

◆ What does *disillusioned* mean?

◆ Have you ever become disillusioned? What happened?

◆ What do you think has happened to Ron Kovic?

Being Alone

12

Solitude: A good place to visit, but a poor place to stay.

—Josh Billings (Peter, 1977, p. 448)

Thinking about solitude gives the students the opportunity to explore their feelings when they are left to themselves and why they may want to escape those feelings.

♦ Do you enjoy being by yourself? Do you ever feel lonely in a crowd? Is being alone the same as being lonely?

♦ Have you ever felt unwanted? Have you ever felt abandoned? How did you react? How did you feel inside?

♦ Do you like the quiet, or do you usually keep a television or radio on at home? Do you use the noise to tune out other people? How do you feel when everything is quiet?

♦ Being in a cave with no lights is supposed to be as dark as any possible experience. What is the blackest darkness you have ever known? What is the most complete darkness you can imagine? Would it be physical or psychological?

Essay Prompt ◆

(Narrative) Tell about the time when you felt most alone or abandoned.

Extension Activity ◆

Go off by yourself to a park or someplace in nature where you can be all alone without distractions.

Video ◆

Iron Will (Schwartz, Palmer, & Haid, 1994) is a story of a young man's fortitude in the face of his father's death. Will participates in a winner-take-all dogsled race to save his family farm as well as his own future. Plenty of adversaries are pitted against the lonesome young man who beats the odds to win the race.

- Would you be willing to fight in a war if you didn't know who or why you were fighting?
- Do you believe people die for a reason?
- Have you ever had anyone tell you they were sorry but you felt they didn't really mean it?
- Do you know what empathy is? Are you an empathetic person?
- When do you feel most alive?
- Have you ever trained for something you really wanted to accomplish?
- What is the longest you've gone without sleeping?
- Why is it a disadvantage to be leading a dogsled race through the early stages of the race?
- Why is the "kid" a gift from God to the reporter?
- Have you ever pushed yourself until you felt you could go no farther?
- Have you ever given up on a goal?
- How did you feel after giving up?
- What would have happened if Will had lost the race?

◆ Related Reading

Gary Paulson's (1987) *Hatchet* tells of a boy's solitary survival (physically and mentally) after a plane crashes in a remote wilderness. Because of his parents' recent separation, the boy has to deal with a multitude of depressing thoughts while he is trying to survive a dangerous situation. Although the reading level is not difficult, the book is written so that it is also appropriate for older students.

- Have you ever been flying in a small plane?

- Are you afraid to fly? Does it make a difference whether you are flying in a jet or a small plane?

- Have you survived a divorce? (If you haven't, have any of your friends?) How did it make you (or your friend) feel?

- Have you ever given a parent the silent treatment? How did you feel when you were doing it? How did you feel afterward?

- Do you think you could successfully land an airplane on your first try? Why or why not?

- What would you think about if you were riding in a plane that was crash landing?

- Have you ever been swarmed by mosquitoes? What happened?

- How important is positive thinking when you are in a difficult situation? How about in the rest of your life?

- Do you ever treat animals as though they were human? Do you think you would treat them as human if you were stuck all by yourself?

- If you were lost in the wild, what would be your greatest difficulty? What would be your greatest fear?

- If you were lost alone in the wilderness, would you try to find your way out or stay where you were?

- Do experts recommend you try to get out of the woods or stay where you are?

Communication

13

No one can make you feel inferior without your consent.
—Eleanor Roosevelt (Bartlett, 1968, p. 981)

How we communicate makes a tremendous difference in our perceptions of the world. Teenagers often have their own way of perceiving and communicating.

- What would the world be like if we couldn't talk? Describe a day in your life if no one could talk.

- Do you know anyone who is hard of hearing? What do you think it feels like to be deaf in our society? If you had to choose between being deaf or blind, which would you choose? Why?

- If someone says something to hurt you, what is your usual reaction? Do you talk to them? Why or why not? If someone says something good to you, what is your usual reaction? Is it easier to react to praise or criticism?

- Television has changed the way our world interacts. How do you think the computer will change the way we communicate? Do you think it will be better or worse than it is now?

◆ Essay Prompt

(Persuasive) Agree or disagree with the statement, "Television is the greatest invention of the 20th century."

◆ Extension Activity

Try learning some sign language, use it in public, and see how different people react.

◆ Video

Renaissance Man (Colleton, Abbot, Greenhut, & Marshall, 1994) stars Danny De Vito as an out-of-work ad salesman who gets a job teaching army recruits who have learning difficulties. Both De Vito and the recruits grow through their relationship. *Hamlet* is the vehicle by which the young soldiers are taught to think. There is one scene with profanity when De Vito is talking to Gregory Hines, who says "Who the F . . . is Lou?" If this scene is removed by fast forwarding, the rest of the movie is well worth watching.

- ◆ Have you ever lost a job? How did that feel?
- ◆ How would you feel if you had to live on welfare?
- ◆ Is the way you say something more important than what you say?
- ◆ How do you feel when someone starts using lingo that you don't understand?
- ◆ Have you ever had a teacher who tried to teach you how to think?
- ◆ What kinds of problems would you give a student to teach him or her how to think?
- ◆ Have you ever been part of a group that was called by derogatory names?
- ◆ Have you ever been accused of not caring about what you do?
- ◆ Why are drill sergeants so important to the military?
- ◆ Have you ever tried rappelling? Would you want to?
- ◆ What do ropes courses teach you?

- Do you "look down" as soon as someone tells you not to?

- What is sarcasm? Why are some people always sarcastic?

- Have you ever memorized poetry?

- What do you think will happen to Hobbs?

- Did you ever feel like you got something you didn't deserve? How did you feel?

- What does the line, "To thine own self be true, and thou canst not then be false to any man," mean?

Related Reading ◆

Romeo and Juliet (see Lamb & Lamb, 1972) has been updated in several recent movies, so many students may have a partial understanding of the story. Because of its timeless message of love intertwined amid gang warfare, it can be an effective means of exploring a number of teen-related issues.

- Why is it so hard to tell someone you love him or her?

- Does the language of Shakespeare make the story more beautiful or just harder to understand?

- What does it tell someone when you blush?

- Have you ever been so involved in a lengthy conversation that time passed without you realizing it?

- Have you ever been stuck in a conversation when time stood still?

- Why are most wars (between gangs or countries) fought?

- Does communication have much to do with the causes of war?

- If you were deeply in love, is there anything your mate could do that would change your feeling for him or her?

- Is there anything he or she could say that could cause you to forgive him or her?

- How does a lack of communication doom Romeo and Juliet?

- If Romeo and Juliet had made their love known earlier, do you think the Capulets and Montagues could have gotten together, or did it take death to open everyone's eyes?

14 Peace

Peace rules the day where reason rules the mind.
— William Collins (Henry, 1945, p. 203)

Teen violence seems to be on the rise, so students have these chances to decide what peace means to the individual and to national interests.

- Do you think countries now are friendlier than they were in the past? Do you think our world will ever become one country like it is in *Star Trek?* Why or why not?

- Do you think teenagers are more violent now than they were in the past? Why or why not? Do you think watching violent television causes more violence? How do you think we could reduce teen violence?

- If somebody picks a fight with you, what choices do you have? If someone confronts you physically and you just walk away, does that make you a coward? What if they call you a coward in front of your friends?

- What does the word *peace* mean to you? What does it mean to be at peace with yourself? How could you have a more peaceful life?

Essay Prompt

(Persuasive) Agree or disagree with the statement, "Teenagers are more violent than they were in the past."

Extension Activity

Watch the movie *Planet of the Apes* (Jacobs & Schaffner, 1968), and compare it to the *Star Trek* vision of Earth hundreds of years from now.

Video ◆

Science fiction movies such as *Star Trek IV: The Voyage Home* give a look at what the world may be in the future. *Star Trek IV* (Bennett & Nimoy, 1986) tells how the crew of the *Enterprise* returns to Earth 300 years from now, and provides a new vantage point for examining our current society. The movie pokes fun at modern profanity that may be objectionable to certain audiences.

- ◆ Do you think it is worth losing one person's life in order to save the lives of many?

- ◆ What would your life be like without emotion?

- ◆ Do you believe animals can have sophisticated intelligence? Why are whales so intriguing to humans?

- ◆ If you could travel through time, would you go forward or backward? Why?

- ◆ Who is the smartest person you know? Why do you consider her or him to be intelligent? Is she or he very emotional?

- ◆ Theoretically, is it possible to go back in time?

- ◆ Do you believe Earth has been visited by creatures from other places or times? Would you tell anyone if you saw a UFO?

- ◆ Do you believe that you have to swear to get people to listen to you? What function does swearing serve in your life?

- ◆ Do you think killing off species of animals could lead to the extinction of humans?

◆ Three hundred years from now, if all the world is united, do you think we will still have a president? Why or why not?

◆ Do you ever think about the end of the world? How do you picture it in your mind?

Giving

15

You give but little when you give of your possessions, it is when you give of yourself that you truly give.

—Kahlil Gibran (Henry, 1945, p. 105)

Giving is often an expectation at certain times of the year. However, adolescence can be a very narcissistic time of life.

- What is the best gift you ever received? How did you show your appreciation for the gift? Is there something you always wanted as a present but didn't get?

- What is the best gift you ever gave someone? Why was that a special gift? Were you anxious before you gave it? What do you enjoy the most, giving gifts to someone special or receiving gifts?

- What do you think of when you think of Christmas or Hanukkah or Kwanzaa? Do you enjoy all the hoopla that goes with the holiday season? Are those holidays becoming too commercialized? Do you think people are friendlier to each other during the holidays?

- What does your family usually do for Christmas or Hanukkah or Kwanzaa? What is your favorite holiday memory? What makes it special for you?

◆ Essay Prompt

(Persuasive) Agree or disagree with the statement, "It doesn't mean much to give a poor person money, you have to give of yourself to make a difference."

◆ Extension Activity

Give away something that you really value (or try giving away some of your time that you would normally save for yourself).

◆ Video

It's A Wonderful Life (Capra, 1946) is the classic story of George Bailey and the difference he makes in the lives of the people in a small town. He sacrifices his dreams for other people. At a particularly low point of his life, an angel shows him what his world would have been like if he hadn't been around.

- ◆ Do you have big plans for your life? What are some?
- ◆ Do you believe there is a higher force in the world that has a plan for your life?
- ◆ How does George give up his life for his family, the building and loan company, his town?
- ◆ What do you give up for your family?
- ◆ What kinds of dreams would you be willing to give up for the love of your life?
- ◆ Do you have ideals or values that you try to live by? What are the three most important ones?
- ◆ Do you feel stuck where you are?
- ◆ What would happen to banks if they ran their business the way George did?
- ◆ Do most companies run their business like Mr. Potter?
- ◆ How would you run you own business, like George or Mr. Potter?
- ◆ What would the world be like if everyone gave up their life for others like George did?
- ◆ Do your parents stand up for you against the school?

◆ What are three ways you have made the members of your family's lives better?

◆ What are three ways the world would be different if you hadn't been born?

◆ Would it be a good idea for everyone to see what the world would be like if they weren't around?

Related Reading ◆

"The Gift of the Magi" (see Hanson, 1948) is O'Henry's classic tale of sacrificial love. A young married couple with very little money gives away their most valued possessions in order to buy gifts for each other. The wife sells her beautiful hair to buy her husband a watch chain; the husband sells his watch to buy his wife a comb. The story is short enough for reluctant readers but profound enough to use as a discussion piece with any age group.

◆ Why is Della upset?

◆ Have you ever cried or yelled as loud as you could when no one else was around? Did that make you feel better?

◆ What are the Dillinghams' most prized possessions?

◆ What are your most prized possessions?

◆ Have you ever given away a prized possession? How did you feel doing that?

◆ Have you ever received a prized possession? Did you value the gift as much as the giver did?

◆ What did Della buy her husband? What did he buy for her?

◆ Why does O'Henry call the Dillinghams the wisest of all givers?

◆ Write your own ending to the story. What do you think will happen to the Dillinghams as they grow old together?

◆ Do you think they will always remember that Christmas?

◆ Did the ending surprise you or did you figure out what was going to happen much earlier in the story?

◆ Do you like stories with surprises or do you like stories that end the way you want them to?

◆ What would you change to update the story of the Dillinghams?

The Future

16

It is a mistake to look too far ahead. The chain of destiny can only be grasped one link at a time.

—Winston Churchill (Safir & Safire, 1982, p. 132)

The beginning of a new year is often a time for looking ahead, something that teenagers often fail to do.

♦ Do you know anyone who makes New Year's resolutions? Do they stick to their resolutions? What are two dreams you have for the future? How are you working to make them come true?

♦ What do you think the world will be like in the year 2020? How about 2050? How will life be different? How will it be the same? Do you think you will still be around in the year 2050?

♦ Scientists now have the ability to clone sheep. Do you believe we should clone animals? Should we clone people? If you could pick certain characteristics of yours that your children would have, would you do it? What characteristics of yours would you not want them to have?

♦ Why are people concerned about the environment and recycling if they won't be around when the world gets too polluted to live in? Do you recycle? Do you ever do things for other people when you know you won't get paid back in some way?

Essay Prompt

(Expository) Compare our world to what you believe the world will be like 100 years from now.

Extension Activity

Get involved in a recycling project.

Video ◆

Michael Keaton plays an overworked husband and father who takes the easy way out in the movie *Multiplicity* (Albert & Ramis, 1996). He pays a scientist to make clones of himself and then pays the consequences. It starts as a good concept piece and deteriorates into the type of movie that appeals to adolescents, but it may not be appropriate for all audiences.

- ◆ Have you ever felt so overwhelmed with your life that you didn't know how you would get out of the situation?

- ◆ What is your first response when people ask you to do something?

- ◆ Would you quit your career to take care of your children? Which is more important to you, a career or a family?

- ◆ Are you the type of person who tries to do everything yourself or do you try to get help?

- ◆ Would you want a clone of yourself?

- ◆ Have you ever had something go so well that you wanted more and more until it backfired on you (or you ate so much of your favorite food that you got sick)?

- ◆ What would be the advantages of having a clone?

- ◆ What would be the disadvantages?

- ◆ What if you got a clone when you were 25 and your clone started out as a baby? Do you think it would become like you because you had the same genes?

- ◆ Are women naturally better (more nurturing) parents than men?

◆ Related Reading

A science fiction story, Lewis Lowry's (1993) Newbery Award winner *The Giver,* is set in a futuristic society that has given up much of its freedom in order to eliminate pain and suffering. A young boy is the designated memory keeper for the entire community because memories contain sadness. The book describes his struggles and the decisions he has to make when he confronts the society's history. There's not a great deal of action, but there is plenty of food for thought and discussion.

- ◆ In certain communes, specialists raise children instead of parents. Do you think that is a good idea? Why or why not? Are day care facilities doing the same thing in our culture?

- ◆ What are your first indications that this society is different from ours?

- ◆ Do you have certain rituals in your own family?

- ◆ Do you think wearing uniforms to school is the first step toward government control of your life? What about gun control by the government?

- ◆ Why would it be important not to have "stirrings" in a controlled society?

- ◆ Should we wait until children are older to give them their names?

- ◆ Why do you have to study history at school?

- ◆ Have you ever been singled out to receive special treatment? How did you feel?

- ◆ Do you think society would run smoother if children's futures were decided ahead of time?

- ◆ Would books be more important to you if they were hard to get?

- ◆ Do you ever think of your life as being without color, in terms of black and white?

- ◆ Would Jonas have had a chance to change his society by staying?

- ◆ What will happen to the community without its memories?

- ◆ What would happen to Jonas if he returned? Write your own ending to the story that includes Jonas's, returning to his society.

Coming of Age

17

Why do you have to be a non-conformist like everybody else?
—James Thurber (Princeton Language
Institute, 1993, p. 90)

The passage into adulthood is a critical time for teenagers. These questions try to prod young people into thinking about what makes a person an adult.

* What is your definition of an adult? How old does someone have to be to be an adult? Do you consider yourself an adult? Why or why not?

* In some older societies, teenagers go through rituals or quests when they are ready to become adults. Some teens would go into the wild for days without food until they had a vision. What type of vision quest or quests would you have young people complete to show they are ready to become adults? Would you ever want to try a vision quest?

* What kinds of markers do we have in our society to show that a person has become an adult? How old do you have to be to do things like drinking or driving a car? Do you think they are good indicators that someone is an adult?

◆ Is having sex an indication that someone is an adult? How about becoming a parent? What responsibilities do you have now? What other responsibilities do you expect to have as an adult?

◆ Essay Prompt

(Narration) Tell about the first time you tried driving (a car, a bike, a motorcycle).

◆ Extension Activity

Go out on your own vision quest to examine if you are ready to reach adulthood (even if you already consider yourself an adult, it is worth the experience).

◆ Video

Dirty Dancing (Gottlieb, Bergstein, & Ardolino, 1987) tells the story of a girl leaving her parents, her way of life, and a place in society for the first love of her life. There are some adult themes so the movie definitely should be previewed, but it does bring up many of the important issues of the passage into adulthood.

◆ Have you ever gone on a vacation with your entire family?

◆ Do you like to dance?

◆ What do you do so you don't feel self-conscious in a new situation?

◆ Would you want a job at a fancy resort?

◆ How can music be a sign of rebellion?

◆ Do you know anyone who has gotten pregnant without wanting to? What did she do?

◆ Do your parents ever go off in their own world and have no idea what you are doing?

◆ Have you ever felt a magic connection the first time you met someone?

◆ What do your parents think of your friends?

- Could a young tough guy like Johnny be a professional dancer in this day and age?

- Most parents feel they know what's best for their child. What do you think? At what age should children start thinking for themselves?

- Have you ever done something just for the money even though you thought it was wrong? How did you feel afterward?

- Have you ever been falsely accused?

- Have you ever stood up for someone even though you got in trouble for doing so?

- How do you think Johnny changes throughout the story?

- How do you think Baby changes?

- Fifteen years from the end of the story, will Baby be known as Baby or Frances?

- Write your own ending to the story, telling what happens to Johnny and Baby.

Related Reading

Gary Paulsen's (1994) novel *The Car* describes a 14-year-old boy's trip across the country with two Vietnam vets. The boy's parents both leave him at the same time. He is left alone at home and decides to rebuild an automobile that is partially finished. He then decides to take off to find a relative several thousand miles away. The story centers on his relationship with a hitchhiker who shows him the ways of the road and leads him toward adulthood. Written simply but touching briefly on themes such as homosexuality, prostitution, gambling, and other "adult" issues, the book may not fit in many traditional school settings but could be effective in some alternative models.

- Would you notice right away if your parents left you? What would you do?

- What do you eat when you are left alone?

- Have you ever made a model? Would you like to try?

- Do your parents like their jobs?

- Do your parents enjoy spending time with each other?

- When you put something together, do you read the instructions, check out the pictures, or just start putting the pieces together? Does that tell you anything about the way you learn?

- What did you get out of the sections where someone was describing what it was like in Vietnam? Could you figure out why these sections were included?

- Do you think obsessions are good or bad? Have you ever been so involved in making something that you forgot about eating or what time it was?

- Have you ever hitchhiked or picked up a hitchhiker?

- What would you take if you were leaving on a cross-country trip?

- What is the longest trip you've ever made?

- Do you take pride in your schoolwork?

- Have you ever felt proud of something you have made?

- Why does Shakespeare say that mercy is twice blessed?

- When you go on a trip, do you try to take the back roads to see the countryside or the main highway to get there as fast as possible?

- Do you drink coffee or something else to get you started in the morning?

- Could you spend your life just wandering from place to place?

- Do you prepare for trips or just throw things together right before you leave?

- Why do you think Waylon says you have to stay hungry in order to learn?

- Do you agree that if you want to learn you have to "study the best"?

- How might Terry's relationship with his parents change?

- How could you rewrite the end of the story?

- If someone gives you a gift, do you feel you owe that person?

Dating

18

Love does not consist of gazing at each other but in looking outward together in the same direction.

—Antoine de St. Exupéry (Peter, 1977, p. 307)

The purpose of these questions is to help students start thinking about their relationships with significant others and the true meaning of love.

- ♦ Who was the first person you had a crush on? What is the first "date" that you ever went on? What was the worst date you've ever been on? What was the best date?

- ♦ What would be your idea of the perfect date? Where would it be? Who would it be with?

- ♦ What characteristics would you look for in someone you want to date? How about someone you want to marry? Would the characteristics be different? How important is physical beauty to you? How important is personality? Intelligence?

- ♦ Would you want the person you marry to be smarter or better looking than you? How would you feel if your spouse made more money than you? What if they were so successful you didn't have to work? How would you feel?

◆ Essay Prompt

Write a poem about the love of your life or about the different loves in your life.

◆ Extension Activity

Draw or find a picture that portrays the same characteristics as a person you would want to marry.

◆ Video

Roxanne (Richmil, Melnick, & Schepisi, 1987) is a retelling of the story of Cyrano de Bergerac. Steve Martin plays a fire chief with a rapier-like nose as sharp as his wit. Daryl Hannah ends up learning the meaning of true love.

- ◆ What is your most distinguishing physical feature? Are you proud or ashamed of it?
- ◆ Have you ever asked out someone who you thought was really beautiful or handsome?
- ◆ What is irony? What is sarcasm? Give an example of each.
- ◆ Do you think people make up for their handicaps by doing other things exceptionally well?
- ◆ Why do we have a stereotype of "dumb" jocks?
- ◆ Why do we have a stereotype that physically attractive people have poor personalities?
- ◆ Why do we have friends ask for dates for us?
- ◆ Do you get nervous talking to members of the opposite sex?
- ◆ Do you ever make fun of yourself?
- ◆ Do you often put yourself down? Why?
- ◆ How can you use humor to get out of a difficult situation?
- ◆ Are looks the first thing that attracts you to someone of the opposite sex?

♦ If you really care for someone, do you see their flaws?

♦ Would you sacrifice your feelings for someone to help a friend?

♦ Could you ever love someone with a nose like the chief's?

♦ What is the nicest thing you've ever said to anyone?

Children

19

Level with your child by being honest. Nobody spots a phony quicker than a child.

—Mary MacCracken (Safir & Safire, 1982, p. 41)

In today's society the distance between being a child and having a child can be very slight.

♦ Do you have any friends with children? Do you know any teenagers with children? How did their lives change after they had a child? How would your life change if you were a parent?

♦ Do you want to have children? Why or why not? How many children would you want? How would you treat your children differently than your parents treated you?

♦ How are you like your parents? How are you unlike your parents? What characteristics of your parents would you like your children to have? What characteristics would you not want them to have?

♦ What do you think is more important for children, the genes they are born with or the way they are brought up? Which do you think had more influence for you? Do you think children who grow up to be addicted to drugs or alcohol learn that behavior from their parents, or is an addiction a disease that is passed on by the parents?

Essay prompt

(Narration) Tell about a vivid memory you have of your childhood.

Extension Activity

Spend an hour with a small child, and see how he or she interacts with the world.

Video ◆

How would you react if you were intelligent, sophisticated, coming into adolescence, lived above a morgue, had a father who was a mortician, felt guilty about causing your mother's death, and had lost your best friend? The story line in *My Girl* (Grazer & Zieff, 1992) deals with all these situations in a humorous, graceful manner. Even with all the tragedy, the movie ends with a positive outlook.

- ◆ Do your parents listen to you?
- ◆ Have you ever seen a corpse? Would you want to?
- ◆ Could you be a makeup artist for corpses?
- ◆ Could you live above a morgue?
- ◆ How do you get your parents' attention?
- ◆ Would you rather be with adults or people your own age?
- ◆ Have you ever tried expressing your innermost thoughts, fears, or self through writing?
- ◆ Do your parents go out on dates?
- ◆ Have you had a friend who got you to do things you wouldn't do by yourself?
- ◆ Is it easier to do things with friends than it is by yourself? Why?
- ◆ What do you do when you are very uncomfortable, surrounded by people you don't know?
- ◆ How do you cope with loss?
- ◆ What could Veda's father have done to help her deal with the loss of her mother?
- ◆ How do your parents show they care for you?
- ◆ How do you show your parents that you care for them?

Old Age

20

Growing old isn't so bad when you consider the alternative.
—Maurice Chevalier (Peter, 1977, p. 356)

In our youth-oriented culture, old age comes quickly. These questions center around the meaning associated with growing old.

- What do you think of when you think of your grandparents? Do you like visiting them? Do they have habits that irritate you? Do you see them very often?

- How do you feel about growing old? What means more to you, your mind or your body? If you could live to be a very old age and could keep either your body or your mind as it is now, which would you keep? Why?

- If you could know when you were going to die, would you want to know? How would you live differently if you knew you were going to die at 20? How would live differently if you knew you would live to be 90 unless you caused your own death by doing something stupid?

- Write your own obituary. What would it say if you were to die tomorrow? What would you want it to say if you lived until you were 80?

Essay Prompt ◆

(Expository) Compare your grandparents with your parents.

Extension Activity ◆

Visit an elderly person or a home for senior citizens. Then examine whether you look at life any differently after talking to them.

Video ◆

A combination of science fiction and a comedic look at aging, *Cocoon* (Zanuck, Brown, & Howard, 1985) features a number of elderly people who are given the chance to regain some youth. An alien culture has left some of its members as cocoons down at the bottom of the ocean. When the aliens return to retrieve the cocoons, they store them in a pool that then gives revitalizing vigor to members of the senior citizens home next door. The movie ends with the elders getting a chance to leave Earth for a long, respected life with the aliens. Some crude language and sexual innuendo means that this movie should definitely be previewed.

- ◆ Why do we ship our elders off to "old folks" homes?
- ◆ Sometimes people who are very old can act like little children. Can you name some of the ways?
- ◆ What are three characteristics we associate with the elderly?
- ◆ What kind of old person do you hope to be?
- ◆ What do we lose by not interacting with our senior citizens?
- ◆ Do you know children who don't interact with their peers? Do you think it is because they are afraid?
- ◆ Would you believe your spouse if your spouse said he or she had seen an alien?
- ◆ How much of old age is mental and how much is physical?
- ◆ Have you ever been left behind?
- ◆ How does the young boy change in the story?
- ◆ Why don't the grandparents tell their daughter what is happening?

- ◆ Would you choose to go in the spacecraft?

- ◆ Do you stick with your decisions?

- ◆ Which older person in the movie is the most like you hope to be at that age?

What Dreams May Come

21

To sleep, perchance to dream; ah, there's the rub, for in that sleep of death, what dreams may come.

—William Shakespeare (Henry, 1945, p. 257)

Thoughts of immortality and suicide intermingle in the teenage mind, so it's good to give them a chance to think about the possibilities of life after death.

* What would a perfect world look like to you? Who would be there? Who wouldn't be there? What kind of climate, terrain, and buildings would you have? What would you be doing? Would you have to work at all? Do you think you would get bored?

* A philosopher wrote that the worst world he could imagine would be one in which he was stuck in a room with the three people who irritated him the most during his life. Who would those people be for you? What would the worst world be that you could imagine?

* Reincarnation is the belief that your soul returns to Earth in another form after you die. What would you return as? Why?

* Think of a painting or photograph that you really like. Describe the picture. Imagine yourself in the picture. What is going on? What kind of feelings do you have when you think of the picture?

◆ Essay Prompt

(Expository) Look at several artists' conceptions of an afterlife. Compare them to each other and to your own conceptions.

◆ Extension Activity

Spend some time in a cemetery. Look at the gravestones. What would you want your gravestone to say?

◆ Video

What Dreams May Come (Simon, Bain, & Ward, 1998) gives a picture of what life after death may look like. Robin Williams stars as a doctor who dies and then deals with the issues with his family that he faced during his lifetime. The movie also focuses on his wife and her subsequent suicide. Graphic scenes of death and frank discussion of suicide may make the film inappropriate for some classrooms.

- Do you see death as an end or a beginning?
- Would you live differently if you thought of death more frequently?
- Do you know what *karma* means?
- Do you believe you get paid back after you die for the bad things you did during your life? How about the good things?
- Do you believe you get paid back (for good or bad) while you are still alive?
- Do you think you will continue to learn and grow as a person after you are dead?
- How would you react if everyone important in your life suddenly died?
- Does suicide ever solve someone's problems?
- Have you ever had to have an animal put to sleep?
- Many people see a white light during near-death experiences. What do you imagine death to be?
- Are you afraid of death?

- Have you ever used writing as therapy?

- Who would you pick as the person to help you through eternity?

- Do you believe you have a soul mate?

- Did you play a lot of games with your parents when you were smaller? Did they let you win?

- Do you think life is harder for people who don't believe there is a life after this one?

Related Reading

Everlasting life after drinking from the fountain of youth is the story in *Tuck Everlasting* (Babbitt, 1975). And for the Tuck family, all is not an eternal joy ride. A young girl discovers their spring of life. The discovery brings up a number of dilemmas that give the reader plenty of food for thought.

- Does August seem like the end of a year to you because school starts soon?

- How does the author's description of Treegap lead the reader to the belief that something strange is about to happen?

- What are the signs that Tuck is unhappy with his life?

- If you lived forever on Earth, would you consider that to be more like heaven or hell?

- Are you afraid when you are alone in the woods or other natural settings?

- If you were stuck on Earth for eternity, what age would you want to be? What would be the worst age to be?

- What do you fear most about dying?

- Would you drink the everlasting water even if you had to live a life like the Tuck family's?

- Would you want to live forever if you would never again see anyone that you knew? How important are your relationships with other people?

22 Money

When I had money everyone called me brother.
—Polish Proverb (Henry, 1945, p. 178)

A dominating theme of adolescence is money, how to get it, how to spend it, and how much importance it has in one's life.

+ Is money the most important thing in our society? If it is, why do you think it is? If it isn't, what do you think is more important?

+ Describe what a day in your life would be like if money wasn't around. How would you get the things you want? What problems would arise? How would you get around those problems?

+ If you won a million dollars (taxfree), what would you do with the money? Would you save any? Would you give any away?

+ Hetty Green inherited $5 million, and by the time her son reached 14 she was worth $25 million. Her son twisted his knee but she would not take him to a doctor because she didn't want to spend the money. He was in pain for 3 years before they dressed up as poor people and went to a doctor. After three visits, the doctor found out who she was and demanded payment. Hetty would not take her son back to the doctor. Two years later, he had to have his leg amputated. When Hetty died, she left her two children $100 million. How would you feel if you were her child? Are 5 years of pain and an amputated leg (not to mention a mother who worries more about money than your well-being) worth a $50 million inheritance?

Essay Prompt

(Persuasive) Agree or disagree with the statement, "Money paves the way to happiness."

Extension Activity

Instead of giving a street person money, offer to buy some food and see how the person reacts.

Video ◆

Greedy (Grazer & Lynn, 1994) starts out with a good premise and brings up a number of issues involving the importance of money and relationships. The film degenerates into slapstick vulgarity that appeals to adolescent humor. It definitely needs previewing, and you may decide to skip the second half of the movie.

- ◆ Do you have any wealthy relations or friends? Do you act differently around them?

- ◆ Would you "kiss up" to an older rich relative?

- ◆ What are your conversations like around the dinner table at home?

- ◆ How would you react if an older relative started living with a much younger person?

- ◆ How would you feel if your spouse were much more successful than you?

- ◆ Do you know anyone who worships money? Can money become a religion?

- ◆ Does wanting money corrupt people?

- ◆ If you were super rich, how could you discover if people really cared about you?

- ◆ Do you want to leave your children an inheritance, or do you plan to spend your money while you have it?

- ◆ How much of your values would you sacrifice for $20 million?

Occupations

23

Better to wear out than to rust out.
—Richard Cumberland (Bartlett, 1968, p. 367)

Deciding on a career field is a major decision of adolescence, although a person's attitude toward work is just as important.

- ◆ Some people believe that you should be paid according to how difficult your job is. What jobs should be paid the most in our society? Why? What jobs are the most overpaid in our society? Why do you think so?

- ◆ How important is pay for you when you think of a future occupation? Would you rather enjoy your job and not get paid much or make lots of money doing something you don't really like?

- ◆ What characteristics are important to you when you think of a future occupation? Would you rather work inside or outside? Alone or with others? Do physical labor or work with your mind?

- ◆ What are three jobs or types of jobs you think you would be good at doing? What would be your dream job? Write a letter or recommendation for yourself to a possible future employer.

Essay Prompt ◆

Complete a résumé or write an interest letter to a possible employer.

Extension Activity ◆

Fill out a career assessment to discover possible career interests.

Video ◆

Much more than a story about an occupation, *My Bodyguard* (Devlin & Bill, 1980) tells about friends, foes, conceptions, and misconceptions at a public high school in New York. Matt Dillon plays a thug who extorts lunch money from most of the boys at school. He meets his match in the new student who hires a huge but misunderstood sophomore as his bodyguard. The movie ends with a fistfight that might not be good modeling, but the main focus is on standing up for oneself.

- ◆ How would you like to live in a hotel?

- ◆ Sometimes the highest paying jobs have the greatest responsibilities. Can you give some examples of jobs that come with big responsibilities?

- ◆ Do you put down other people?

- ◆ Have you ever stood up to a bully? How did that feel?

- ◆ Would you want a job where you tell a bunch of people what to do?

- ◆ Does your father know how old you are? Is he involved in your life? How would you feel if he called school to tell them a bully was picking on you?

- ◆ Have you ever taken a problem to a higher authority (parent, teacher, principal) and had it backfire on you?

- ◆ Do you know any students who are surrounded by rumors because no one really knows much about them?

- ◆ Would you rather work with people or machines?

- ◆ How would you feel if you could rebuild a motorcycle?

- Why do you think a teenager like Ricky Linderman comes to school?

- What makes someone tough in your eyes?

- Have you ever gotten someone else to take care of your problems for you?

◆ Related Reading

Cushman's (1995) award-winning *Midwife's Apprentice* is the story of an orphaned girl who will do anything for a warm place to stay. It is really the story of perseverance in the face of long odds as she struggles to find a place in her community. She studies the work of her boss, the midwife, until she can do the job as well as her master, even though her master treats her poorly.

- Have you ever saved an animal? How did that feel?

- Do you think most people choose the job they have because they really enjoy that line of work, or do they get the job because of other circumstances (they need the money, it's offered to them by someone they know, etc.)?

- How can you work now to make sure you get the job you want?

- What's the worst job you can imagine?

- How would you feel if you were a teacher and your student (apprentice) became better at the job than you were?

- How would you feel if you were the student and you became better than your master?

- Is it the job of students to go beyond their teacher?

- How would you react to a boss who never praises you and only points out your mistakes?

- Have you ever had a teacher like that?

- Are you superstitious? Do you have any specific superstitions?

- Have you ever felt you were too dumb to do a job?

- Can you think of any jobs nowadays that rely on tricks and deceptions?

- Why are people returning to traditional practices like using herbs and midwives?

Emotions

24

Never apologize for sharing feelings. When you do so you apologize for truth.

—Benjamin Disraeli (Safir & Safire, 1982, p. 126)

Adolescence tends to be a time of great emotional highs and lows, good as well as bad. It is always a good idea to examine them objectively when passions are subdued.

+ Do you consider yourself a violent person? What situations make you angry? Who makes you angry? Can you feel your anger rising? Are you able to calm yourself down?

+ When was the last time you cried in front of someone? When was the last time you cried when you were all alone? When was the last time you saw your mother cry? How about your father? Why is it so hard for men to express emotion in our society? Would you consider a guy who cries less of a man? Why?

+ What kinds of things make you anxious? Do you ever start to sweat when you are anxious? Have you ever been so anxious that you decided not to do something you had planned on doing? Do you think a little anxiety is good?

+ What kinds of things make you happy? What is the happiest you've been in the past year? Is your main purpose in life trying to find happiness or something else? If it is something else, what is it? Why?

◆ Essay Prompt

(Poetry) Write a poem using descriptions of emotions or situations that cause certain emotions.

◆ Extension Activity

Find a picture or painting (or draw a picture) that elicits certain emotions, and try to figure out what it is about the picture that brings out those emotions.

◆ Video and Related Reading

The movie *The Color Purple* (Spielberg, 1985) describes a woman's traumatic life as she grows through abusive relationships. The book, written by Alice Walker (1982), also contains some frank discussions of abuse and sexual relations. Both the book and the movie are powerful stories but need to be previewed for appropriateness for specific students.

- ◆ Does abuse destroy Celie's spirit?

- ◆ Do people stay in abusive relationships because they have poor self-esteem?

- ◆ Why was the ability to read and write so important to Celie? Is it important to you?

- ◆ Is Nettie stronger than Celie because she decides to leave, or is Celie stronger because she stays?

- ◆ How is Sofia's relationship to Harpo different than Celie's relationship to Albert? How do the relationships change?

- ◆ Can you go to your father when you have a problem?

- ◆ What does Shug do for Celie?

- ◆ Who would you say was the most important person in building your self-esteem?

- ◆ What does having a baby do for a teenage mother's self-esteem?

◆ How does being a woman (or a minority) affect Celie's self-worth?

◆ What emotions do you think Celie feels as she leans over Albert's throat with a razor in her hand?

◆ How does Celie grow as a person?

25 Crimes

"When I see the 10 most wanted lists . . . I always have this thought: If we'd made them feel wanted earlier, they wouldn't be wanted now."
—Eddie Cantor (Peter, 1977, p.143)

Difficulties with the law dominate the lives of many teenagers whether they are directly involved or just have friends who get in trouble.

- Should parents be held responsible when their children commit crimes? At what age should children be held responsible for their own actions? If parents had to pay for the damage their children cause, do you think it would reduce crime? Why?

- Do you feel safe at school? How can schools be made safer? What would you do to a student who threatens another student? How about a student who brings a weapon to school? Or one who punches another student? Does age matter?

- Have you ever been arrested? Almost arrested? Hassled by the police? Do you think police discriminate against teenagers? How about other minorities?

- Have you ever been locked up or forced to stay in your room for any length or time? What did you do? How did you feel while you were there? What if you had to face a long stretch of solitary confinement?

Essay Prompt ◆

(Persuasive) Agree or disagree with the statement, "Parents should be held responsible for their child's actions."

Extension Activity ◆

Go to a trial and find out how the justice system really works.

Video ◆

George Kennedy and Paul Newman star as chain gang convicts in *Cool Hand Luke* (Carroll & Rosenberg, 1967). Newman plays a free spirit who refuses to bow to the authority of the system. What they have is a failure to communicate. Except for one scene of the prisoners ogling a woman washing her car, there is very little objectionable material, especially compared to more recent R-rated prison movies.

- ◆ Have you ever known anyone who got into trouble just for the fun of it?

- ◆ Why do the guards wear mirrored sunglasses?

- ◆ Would you rather do hard labor in the hot sun or sit in a cell all day long?

- ◆ Why do the guards insist on being called "boss"?

- ◆ What term do you use for someone you respect?

- ◆ Do you know what "passive resistance" means? Have you ever tried it?

- ◆ How can you beat someone who won't quit?

- ◆ How does Luke get his nickname? Why can "nothin'" be a cool hand?

- ◆ What can you learn about Luke from his mother's visit?

- ◆ How can making a game out of a difficult situation make it bearable?

- When does Luke start trying to escape? Why do you think he starts?

- Have you ever had a "failure to communicate" with one of your teachers or someone else in authority?

- Why is Luke such a danger to the warden and the guards?

♦ Related Reading

Newbery Award winner *Holes* (Sachar, 1998) tells the story of Stanley Yelnats and his family. Stanley is wrongly accused, sentenced, and sent to a detention camp at the edge of a dry lake in Texas. His family history and the history of everyone involved in the story are somehow tied to the present and the adventure of Stanley's eventual freedom from the camp. The book is easy to read but has complicated plot lines. It should appeal to almost everyone.

- What does the line, "the warden owns the shade," mean?

- How would you feel after 8 hours on a school bus?

- Why is Camp Lake the perfect spot for a detention facility?

- What does his nickname tell you about each boy? Have you ever earned a nickname?

- Would you choose a work camp or jail if you had the choice?

- What did you think all the holes were for when you first read about them?

- What's the most refreshing swim or shower you can remember?

- How did X-ray get to be the leader of the group?

- Is there a pecking order in your classroom?

- Do you believe in curses?

- How do you gain or lose prestige in the eyes of your friends?

- How does Stanley's plan with the gold tube backfire?

- What part do the onions play in the story?

- What part does prejudice play in the story of Sam and Kate Barlow?

- What does learning to read and write do for Zero?

- When was the last time you made a decision without thinking?

- How do all the pieces of Stanley's story fit together at the end (the Thumb, the onions, the lizards, the shoes, his family, and Zero)?

Punishments

26

We enact many laws that manufacture criminals, and then a few that punish them.

—Benjamin Tucker (Henry, 1945, p. 52)

What effect, if any, does punishment have on our young people in the criminal justice system, and is there a system that might be more effective?

- Do you believe in capital punishment? If you believe in it, what would someone have to do to deserve it? If someone related to you was murdered, would that change how you feel?

- Is capital punishment a deterrent to people who commit murders? Are strict prison sentences a good deterrent for people who commit crimes? Should prisons be tougher on the prisoners? Do you think that would slow down crime?

- More and more teenagers are being treated as adults when they commit violent crimes. Do you think that is a good idea? If a teenager kills someone, should he or she be treated as an adult? Should he or she be executed? How about a 10-year-old? How about an 8-year-old? How or why should a young person be treated differently?

> ◆ Should prisons or juvenile facilities be designed to punish criminals or to rehabilitate them? If your job was to rehabilitate young criminals, what would you do for them?

◆ Essay Prompt

(Persuasive) Agree or disagree with the statement, "We should abolish capital punishment in this country because it is expensive (because of all the appeals) and doesn't do any good."

◆ Extension Activity

Visit a jail or juvenile facility, and imagine what it would be like to stay there.

◆ Video

Tom Hanks and Denzel Washington star as lawyers taking on a giant law firm in *Philadelphia* (Saxon & Demme, 1993). Hanks sues his firm because they fire him once they find out he has AIDS. The movie covers much more than our judicial system and probably fits better under the category of "Equality." It covers some adult themes that may not be appropriate in some school situations.

> ◆ Do we punish people in our society just because they are different?
>
> ◆ What does *innocuous* mean?
>
> ◆ Have you ever met anyone with AIDS? What did you think about that person?
>
> ◆ Do you know any homosexuals? How do you react around them? What is the typical stereotype of a homosexual? Is it deserved?
>
> ◆ Do lawyers deserve their reputation as people who work around the system to get guilty parties out of trouble?
>
> ◆ What is discrimination? Do you discriminate against anyone? Have you ever been discriminated against?
>
> ◆ Would your parents back you up no matter what you did? Have you ever done anything where they didn't back you up?

◆ Do you have friends who would back you up no matter what you did?

◆ Do you believe there are "layers of truth" or only one truth?

◆ Why is this story set in Philadelphia?

◆ Would you say most people in this country are prejudiced against homosexuals? Why are they so despised?

Cliques and Gangs

27

We forfeit three-fourths of ourselves in order to be like other people.
—Arthur Schopenhauer (Peter, 1977, p. 267)

Gathering in groups is a rite of adolescence that very few teens are able to resist.

- Why do you think gangs are so popular now? What is your definition of a gang member? What do they look like? What do they do?

- Do you know any gang members? Many cities would like to reduce the number of teenagers who hang out in gangs. Do you think they can be successful? What would you do if it were your job to reduce the number of gang members in your city?

- What kinds of gangs or cliques are there at traditional high schools? Describe some of them. How do the members dress? What do they do that sets them apart from everyone else?

- Were you ever a member of a clique? Is there a certain clique you'd like to belong to? If you could create you own clique, what would it be like? Who would be in it? What would you do that would set you apart?

Essay Prompt ◆

(Expository) Describe the different cliques at a traditional high school in your town.

Extension Activity ◆

Try talking to someone who is in a different clique than you normally hang out in, and see how he or she reacts.

Video and Related Reading ◆

The Outsiders was both S. E. Hinton's (1967) first book and her first of many that dealt with teens outside the social norm. The movie (*The Outsiders*; Roos, Fredrickson, & Coppola, 1983) featured a number of future stars as Ponyboy, Darry, Dally, and the gang from the poor side of town. They battle the Socs for territory and the interest of a girl, and one of the Socs dies. Ponyboy then suffers the consequences and learns from his experiences. Hinton wrote the book as a 16-year-old, so it has a great deal of interest and relevance to certain teens.

- ◆ Do you have friends who are smart but don't do much in school because they want to fit in with their social group?

- ◆ Are there groups of students who hang out together at your school that aren't really considered gangs but could be?

- ◆ Has anyone ever "attacked" you because of the way you look?

- ◆ Is it impossible to please your parents?

- ◆ What personal dreams would you be willing to give up to help your family?

- ◆ Have you ever liked a girl (or guy) you thought was "too good for you"? What did you do?

- ◆ Do you know anyone who is pretty much ignored by his or her parents?

- ◆ Have you ever run away from a scary situation? What happened?

- ◆ Have you ever turned yourself in after doing something wrong?

- ◆ Does doing something heroic make up for doing something wrong?

- ◆ How will Johnny's parents change after what happened to their son?

- ◆ In 10 years, what do you think will have happened to Pony? How about Darry and the other members of the group? How will they be different than the Socs? What will happen to Cherry?

Uniqueness

28

Know, first, who you are; and then adorn yourself accordingly.
—Epictetus (Princeton Language
Institute, 1993, p. 80)

Many young people are trying to make a statement about who they are but need to think more about what they are really trying to say.

♦ What can people tell about you from the way you dress or look? Do you dress like a certain group? Do people judge you by the way you look? Do you judge others by the way they look? What would you think about a high school boy who wore a tie to school for no apparent reason?

♦ What do you think about wearing a uniform to school? Would wearing a uniform eliminate any problems at school? If you could make up your own uniform (one that you would be willing to wear every day), what would it look like?

♦ In what ways are you similar to most teenagers in our society? How about the way you dress, the way you talk, or what you do out of school?

♦ What makes you different from most teenagers in our society? Are you proud of your differences, or do you try to hide them?

◆ Essay Prompt

(Expository) Compare yourself to the "average" teenager. How are you similar? How are you different?

◆ Extension Activity

Try dressing noticeably different than the way you normally dress, and see how people react to you.

◆ Video

School Ties (Jaffe, Lansing, & Mandel, 1992) tells the story of a Jewish quarterback who gets the opportunity to spend his senior year at an exclusive Catholic prep school. None of the students know he is Jewish, and he slowly backs away from any signs of his heritage. The movie brings out many examples of prejudice and the survival techniques of minorities in this country.

- ◆ Do you think the prejudices in our country have changed over the past 40 years?

- ◆ Why is going to chapel unusual for David Green? Is he turning his back on his beliefs when he takes off his Star of David necklace?

- ◆ Can music become a sign of rebellion?

- ◆ Which is more important, sports or religious rules? Is it worth breaking religious traditions to play sports?

- ◆ Are sports a religion to some people?

- ◆ Do you learn better if you know you will be put on the spot by a teacher during class or if you know you can relax?

- ◆ How important are your grades to you?

- ◆ Have you ever been jealous of someone else's success? What did you do?

- ◆ Are the adults at St. Matt's any less prejudiced than the students? How about the football coach? Where does he fit in?

- ◆ Why is the Nazi cross such a vulgar sign of prejudice?

- If you saw someone you didn't like cheat on a test, would you turn that person in?

- Why is the history teacher so intent on finding the cheater?

- How would you react if you found out someone in your class was cheating?

Related Reading

Night, by Elie Wiesel (1960), is the story of an adolescent Jew growing up in Transylvania during World War II. It is a powerful autobiography that can give students insights into the unique experience of Jewish ancestry and tradition. It can easily be used in conjunction with *School Ties* in the "Equality," "Coming of Age," or "Being Alone" sections.

- Why did Moshe the Beadle come back?

- Why didn't the people want to listen to him?

- Do you ever ignore bad news? Does it work?

- What was a ghetto? Do we still have ghettos?

- Do people naturally hope for the best?

- How has the history of the Jews helped them persevere?

- How would you feel standing in front of someone who could decide if you would live or die simply by pointing a finger?

- Would you continue to hope for the best even through the terrible reality of a concentration camp?

- What traditions did the Jews hold on to even through the camps?

- Why do we ignore stories of the deaths of thousands of people in far-off lands but become mortified by the death of someone we know?

- Why didn't the Jews try to resist even if it meant their death?

- Would you fight for your own life even at the expense of your family?

- How would you feel if you survived the Holocaust and none of your family did?

- Would you live your life differently if you had survived an experience like the Holocaust? How would you live differently?

29 Equality

I have a dream that one day this nation will rise up and live out the true meaning of its creed: we hold these truths to be self-evident, that all men are created equal.

—Martin Luther King Jr. (Princeton Language Institute, 1993, p. 152)

There are few subjects that get teenagers as adamant as that of gender equity, but an equally important issue is that of ethnic equality in our society.

- Who has it harder in our society, men or women? Why? How do you think the roles of men and women in our society have changed over the past 100 years?

- Do you think it was easier when people had predetermined roles? (Men worked, paid the bills, women stayed at home with the children.) Why do you think we have more divorces than we did 100 years ago? How do you think roles will change in the next 50 years?

- India has a caste system where people can't marry or hold a job outside their caste. Does the United States have an informal caste system? Why or why not?

◆ Which ethnic groups have it toughest in the United States? The United States used to be called a melting pot. Would you say it still is? What was good about the United States being a melting pot? What was bad?

Essay Prompt

(Persuasive) Agree or disagree with the statement, "Men have life easier in today's society."

Extension Activity

Look up your family history to see where you came from and to which ethnic groups you belong.

Video

A League of Their Own (Abbott, Greenhut, & Marshall, 1992) is the true story of a women's baseball league that was started during World War II. Many of the male professional players left the country as members of the armed forces, which opened the door for the women. The movie gives a number of examples of gender bias, but it is also about a love of sports and about family relationships. Students will recognize a number of stars, including Madonna, Rosie O'Donnell, Geena Davis, and Tom Hanks.

◆ How does the offer to play pro baseball contain prejudice for the women?

◆ Does the end justify the means?

◆ Does more freedom for women lead to problems in our society?

◆ How have the roles of women and men changed since World War II?

◆ How did the war help lead to those changes?

◆ Should men who play pro sports be given etiquette lessons?

◆ Have you ever had a coach, teacher, or some other authority figure who just didn't care what you did?

- How are the promotions of the female players demeaning? Do pro players still do demeaning commercials?

- Should pro athletes of today have chaperons? Should they be held responsible for their actions outside the arena of sport?

- Have you ever tried swing dancing? Would you like to?

- Once someone has experienced freedom, is it possible to put that person back in bondage?

- Women tennis stars earn the same as men, but women golfers and basketball players don't. Is that unfair?

◆ Related Reading

Sounder (Armstong, 1969) and *Black Like Me* (Griffin, 1960) give two perspectives on the same issue, that of racial equality (or lack thereof) in the southern part of the United States. *Sounder* is a Newbery Award winner written for a young audience, but it gives a starkly depressing picture of a sharecropper's life. It also reiterates the importance and hope that comes with education. *Black Like Me* is a sociological look at what it meant to be black in the 1950s. A novelist, John Howard Griffin, darkens his skin pigment and then travels through the South, giving us an amazing look at prejudice from an unusual vantage point.

- How is life different for the blacks in the story than it is now?

- Do you think life has changed very much for the whites in our society?

- Why do you think life has changed for minorities during the past 30 years?

- What part did education play in bringing about those changes?

- Do you think prejudice was any different depending on which part of the country you lived in? Do you think where you live makes any difference now?

- What are some examples of prejudice that you still see in our country?

- What is an Uncle Tom? Have you ever acted like an Uncle Tom?

- Why do you think blacks (for the most part) simply accepted their fate until the 1950s and 1960s?

- Would it have helped them to fight back?

- How was the plight of the blacks in our country similar to that of the Jews?

- Do you consider yourself to be prejudiced?

- How does someone's skin color affect the way you view him or her?

- Can you stop yourself from being prejudiced? How?

30 Fame

A celebrity is a person who works hard all his life to be known, then wears dark glasses to avoid being recognized.
— Fred Allen (Princeton Language Institute, 1993, p. 167)

Our society is one that gravitates toward the famous, then vilifies them for not living up to our expectations.

- If someone were to make an autobiographical movie about you, which actor or actress would you want to portray you? Why? What other actors would you want playing important parts in the movie? What would the main story line be about?

- Would you want to be so famous that you'd be recognized every time you walked down the street? What would be the perks of being that famous? What would be the drawbacks of being that famous? What would you want to be famous for doing?

- Professional basketball player Charles Barkley has said that he is not a role model. What is meant by a "role model"? Do you think pro athletes are or should be role models? Who is a role model in our society? Why do you think so? Can someone be a role model for something bad?

- Do you have any role models (people you pattern yourself after or look up to)? Do you think you are or could be a role model? Do you think there is more pressure on you if someone looks up to you? Would you want that kind of pressure?

Essay Prompt ♦

(Persuasive) Agree or disagree with the statement, "Pro athletes are role models whether they want to be or not."

Extension Activity ♦

Tell (or write a letter to) someone whom you consider to be a role model that you respect him or her and why you consider that person someone that deserves to be emulated.

Video and Related Reading ♦

Malcolm X is the story of a man who changes his life around from one of corruption and pleasure seeking to one of religion and high moral standards. Both the movie (*Malcolm X*; Worth & Lee, 1992) and the book (*The Autobiography of Malcolm X*; Haley & Malcolm X, 1964) can be effective vehicles for teaching students about an important cultural figure.

- ♦ Malcolm says that people swear only because they don't have the words to express themselves. Do you agree? Why do people swear?

- ♦ How do people use their hair to express themselves?

- ♦ What is the significance of Red trying to straighten his hair?

- ♦ What is the Ku Klux Klan?

- ♦ Do you know students who pretend to like their teacher? Why do they do it?

- ♦ Why was Joe Louis an important figure to African Americans?

- ♦ Do you know any racially mixed couples? What problems do they encounter?

- ♦ Do you know anyone who really turned his or her life around after getting caught for an illegal activity?

- ♦ Do you know anyone who belongs to a different religion?

- What did his faith in Allah do for Malcolm?

- Would you be willing to participate in illegal activities if it meant easy money, even though you could get easily caught and end up in jail?

- Would you be willing to participate in illegal activities if it was for a higher cause, like for your political or spiritual beliefs?

- How did going to prison help turn Malcolm's life around?

- Malcolm learns from reading the dictionary while he is in prison. Have you ever tried reading the dictionary to learn something besides simply how to spell a word? What else can you learn from the dictionary?

- What did Elijah Muhammad do to help Malcolm? What did he do that eventually turned Malcolm against him?

- Muslims believe that a man should be much older than his wife when they get married. Why do you think they believe that is a good idea?

- Would you consider marrying someone who is 15 years older than you? Why or why not?

- Do you think Malcolm was a good family man?

- How did his relationship to Martin Luther King Jr. change?

- What is a pilgrimage?

- Every Muslim hopes to make a pilgrimage to Mecca in his or her lifetime because it is a holy city. Are there people in the United States who try to make pilgrimages to "holy" places? What would those places be?

- Are there places you would like to visit that are especially important to you?

- In Muslim countries, women have a definite place (either in the home or behind a veil). Would you want to live in a Muslim country or household?

- Why do Malcolm's radical friends feel he has betrayed them?

- Why did Malcolm go ahead with his speech even though he knew something bad was likely to happen? What would you have done in his place?

- What do you think happened to Malcolm's radical friends?

- Do you think Malcolm was an important figure in U.S. history? Why?

Decisions

31

Don't be afraid to take a big step when one is indicated. You can't cross a chasm in two small steps.

—David Lloyd George (Safir & Safire, 1982, p. 76)

Teens going into adulthood face many life-changing decisions, so it's a good idea to get them thinking about how and why they make important decisions.

♦ What is your favorite noise? What is your least favorite noise? What is your favorite smell? What is your least favorite smell? How did you decide on your answers? Do you just write the first thing that comes into your mind, or do you compare different answers and decide which is best?

♦ What are the typical decisions you make in a day? How do you make most of your choices? Do you use logic or gut instincts? Does the importance of the decision make a difference?

♦ What is the biggest decision you have made in your life so far? How did you make it? Was it a good or bad decision? What are some other major decisions you will have to make in the coming years? How do you expect to make those decisions?

♦ Do you feel like you have many choices in your life or not so many? Why or why not? How could you get more choices? Do you feel like you have much control over what happens in your life? How could you gain more control?

◆ Essay Prompt

(Expository) Describe the biggest decision you have ever had to make and how it changed your life.

◆ Extension Activity

Think about an important decision that you have to make. Write down all the pros and cons of each choice, and then see if you make a logical decision or an intuitive one.

◆ Video

Benny and Joon (Arnold, Roth, & Chechik, 1993) is the story of a young man who takes care of his psychologically unstable sister after their parents die in a car wreck. Joon connects with an oddball drifter who is gifted in the art of pantomime but is deficient in many other areas. Benny wants to control Joon at the expense of his own personal life, but finally realizes that he has to let her make her own decisions and let her deal with the consequences.

- ◆ What does it mean to "need" someone?
- ◆ What does the saying "When the boat comes ashore, the sea has spoken" mean?
- ◆ What is a metaphor?
- ◆ Have you ever had to take siblings with you when you didn't want to? How did you feel about it?
- ◆ Would you be willing to take care of a needy sibling or parent for the rest of your life? Why or why not?
- ◆ How do we decide that someone is mentally ill?
- ◆ Do you make most of your decisions for yourself or for others?
- ◆ Has there been a turning-point event in your life (like the death of Benny and Joon's parents) that forced you to make a difficult decision?

- Do you put off making important decisions as long as possible?

- Have you ever decided to run away from home?

- What is the one thing you would take with you if you did run away?

- How do you decide how much you care for someone?

Dreaming

32

Believe that life is worth living and your belief will create the fact.
—William James (Bartlett, 1968, p. 794)

Adolescence is a time of oversleeping, sleeping over, and dreaming (both awake and asleep) about how life could be better.

- Do you spend much time daydreaming? What do you like to think about? Where do you usually daydream? Do you blank out sometimes when people are talking to you or lecturing at you? What do you think about?

- Have you ever tried meditation? Try to focus on something for 5 minutes. See if you can empty your mind of all your usual thoughts. After 5 minutes write down what you experienced.

- Do you like to sleep in as long as you can on the days you don't have to get up? Do you set an alarm, or do your parents wake you up on the days you do have to get up? How late do you usually stay up? Do you feel like you get enough sleep on most nights?

- Do you usually remember your dreams? Do you have a recurring dream? Do you remember any particularly vivid dreams? Do you wish you remembered more of your dreams?

Essay Prompt ◆

(Narrative) Tell about your most vivid dream.

Extension Activity ◆

Write down your dreams for a week. If you usually don't remember your dreams, set your alarm clock for 5 minutes earlier than usual and write down whatever you remember as soon as you wake up.

Video ◆

Kevin Costner builds a baseball park and "they come" in *Field of Dreams* (Gordon & Robinson, 1989). He hears voices and obeys their messages, no matter how unreasonable. Players return from the dead to fulfill their dreams on Costner's field. Besides "Sports" and "Dreaming," the story also addresses persevering in the face of logical expectations.

- ◆ Have you ever followed your intuition even though it wasn't the logical thing to do?

- ◆ Who would you say believes in you?

- ◆ Who or what do the voices represent in the movie?

- ◆ What does baseball represent to the doctor?

- ◆ Do you consider yourself more similar to Ray (a dreamer) or Mark (a realist)? Why?

- ◆ What would you think of your father if he heard voices? What if he built a ballpark or did something else unusual because of the voices?

- ◆ What would have happened if Ray had not listened to the voices?

- ◆ What would you tell your parents if they told you they were listening to voices to make their decisions?

- ◆ Who do you think should determine what books should be read in school?

- ◆ Do people lose their passion for life as they grow older?

- ◆ Why do you think a cornfield represents life after death?

Television and Movies

33

Television has proved that people will look at anything rather than each other.

—Ann Landers (Princeton Language Institute, 1993, p. 437)

However dismal the prospect might be, there is perhaps no greater influence in the lives of young people today than that of the media.

- What are your favorite television shows? What is it you like about them? Why do you usually watch television? What kind of influence does television have on our society? What kind of influence has television had on you?

- What would you do if you didn't have television? Have you ever gone a long time without watching it? How is listening to the radio different from watching television? Why are music videos so popular?

- What kinds of movies do you like? Why do you usually go to a movie . . . to be with your friends? . . . to see the movie? . . . to go someplace on a date? Why do people like to go to movies for a date?

106

• What are your top four favorite movies? What was so enjoyable about them? Which one would you pick as the best of all?

Essay Prompt ◆

(Expository) Compare your favorite television show to your favorite movie. How are they similar? How are they different?

Extension Activity ◆

Try going without television for a week.

Video ◆

The Truman Show (Rudin & Weir, 1998) tells the story of a young man whose entire life has been a television show but without his knowledge. Jim Carey plays Truman, who slowly begins to understand that he isn't in control of his life. He gradually takes control and finally breaks out of the television studio.

• Have you ever felt someone was watching you that you couldn't see?

• What are some early indications for Truman that his world isn't real?

• Would you watch a television show like *Truman?*

• Some people are now putting a video camera in their room and putting their life on an Internet Web site and charging people to watch. Would you pay to watch?

• Have you ever been betrayed by your best friend? How did you feel?

• Would you get bored working on a television show, doing the same thing day after day?

• Would you make a good actor or actress?

• Do you ever feel like your world is unreal?

• Do you ever feel like you are not in control of your life?

• What are the psychological ways that Truman is manipulated?

- How does television control us?

- Would you enjoy manipulating someone's life like the director of the show did to Truman?

- Do you think animals would rather have an easy life in a cage or live in the wild with all of the dangers and a shorter life? How about people?

- What do you do when your favorite show is taken off the air?

- Do you think they will get another Truman for a new show?

Experiences

34

I am not afraid of storms for I am learning to sail my ship.
—Louisa May Alcott (Princeton Language
Institute, 1993, p. 161)

Part of growing up is taking on new experiences and new challenges
and evaluating what it was that made them difficult.

- Describe the hardest thing you have ever had to do or endure physically. What made it so difficult? Was it a single moment or something that was drawn out over a long time? How did you feel during the experience? How did you feel when it was over?

- Describe the hardest thing you have ever done intellectually. Does school challenge your mind? Do you like to be challenged and required to think? Why or why not?

- What was the hardest thing you have had to deal with emotionally? Was it something you caused yourself or something that someone did to you? How did you deal with it? Would you deal with it the same way if it happened again?

- If you had to compare your physical, intellectual, and emotional sides, which would you say is the strongest? Which is the weakest? In which area do you like to be challenged? What do you try to stay away from?

◆ Essay Prompt

(Narration) Tell about the hardest thing you have ever done.

◆ Extension Activity

Try to find an activity that challenges you on all levels (such as a ropes course) and see what it is that you like or dislike about those challenges.

◆ Video

The movie *White Fang* (Powell & Kleiser, 1991) is a retelling of Jack London's (1981) story. As such, it concentrates on the human characters, especially the young man who befriends White Fang. All of London's work is the stuff of which dreams are made, adventures created, and life experienced, and thus *White Fang* would be appropriate for this section as well as the "Fears," "Being Alone," or "Decisions" sections.

- Have you ever felt completely lost in a new situation? What did you do?

- What do you do anytime you feel completely overwhelmed?

- Have you ever trusted complete strangers? Did it work out for you?

- What's the coldest you have ever been?

- Would you go searching after a treasure under trying circumstances even if there was only a one in a hundred chance you would find it? How about one in a thousand?

- Do you think treasure hunters really worry about what they find, or do they just enjoy the search?

- How important are promises to you?

- If you had to go on a great adventure, whom would you want as your partner?

- Could you last for an entire winter in a one-room cabin? What would you need to help you survive mentally?

- Have you ever helped a wounded or sick animal?

- What is the hardest work you have ever done?

◆ Have you ever done something that made you feel bad but was really the best thing to do (like letting an animal return to the wild)?

Related Reading ◆

"To Build a Fire" (London, 1981) describes the ultimate experience, that of the struggle for life against the onslaught of death. A man traveling through Alaska's backcountry falls through thin ice on a day of super-cold temperatures. He then fights to build a fire that will determine whether he lives or dies.

◆ How does London set the scene for a struggle in the first paragraph?

◆ What is a "chechaquo?" Have you ever felt you were a chechaquo?

◆ How does London demonstrate how cold it was?

◆ Why is it good to eat a lot of fat in cold weather?

◆ How was the animal's instinct better than the man's intellect?

◆ What does *rationalize* mean? How does the man rationalize his traveling through the bitter cold?

◆ Why is the power of observation so important when traveling through nature? Has modern man lost some of that power? Has modern man lost other senses or animal instincts?

◆ Why does the man choose to travel along the creek bed even though it is such a dangerous place to be?

◆ Why is constant movement important in such cold temperatures?

◆ What mistakes did the man make?

◆ What would have been different if he had been traveling in this day and age?

◆ How would you react if you knew you were going to die but there was nothing you could do about it? Would you continue to struggle to live?

◆ Was there anything else the man could have done?

35 Famous Dates

Tomorrow life is too late: live today.
—Marcus Valerius Martialis
(Henry, 1945, p. 286)

Sometimes it is a good idea to make the associations between our actions and whether we had a successful day or an unsuccessful one.

♦ On December 7, 1941, President Roosevelt said it was a day that would live in infamy. Do you know what happened on that day? Do you have certain days in your life that will live in infamy? What happened?

♦ Have you had a really good day when everything seemed to go right? What happened? What would the perfect day for you be like?

♦ What is your favorite day of the week? Why? What do you usually do on that day? How does that change during the summer?

♦ Are there certain days every year that you dread, like the first day of school or April Fool's Day? Are there certain days that you look forward to each year, like New Year's Eve or your birthday? What important dates would you like to celebrate in your life as you grow older? Do you remember anniversaries? Are they important to you?

Essay Prompt ◆

(Narrative) Tell about the best day you've ever had, the worst day you've ever had, or make up a story about the best day you've ever had.

Extension Activity ◆

Go through a calendar and mark dates you really anticipate (in a positive way) in blue, mark the dates that you dread in red, and see how many of each you end up with.

Video ◆

Groundhog Day (Albert & Ramis, 1993) stars Bill Murray as a television weatherman who gets stuck living the same day over and over again. Although the premise seems absurd, the movie brings out a number of philosophical issues, such as: What would we do with an immortal life? How important are relationships in our lives? What enjoyment do we obtain by serving other people, and what pleasure do we gain from simply living for the moment?

- ◆ How important is your attitude when you have a job to do?

- ◆ How do you usually wake up (alarm clock, your parents, on your own)?

- ◆ If there was one day of your life you could live again, would it be a really good day or would you want to go back to a bad day and try to change something that you did?

- ◆ How would you react if each day seemed to repeat itself?

- ◆ Do you ever feel so bored that it seems as if every day does repeat itself?

- ◆ Who do you turn to when you really need help?

- ◆ How does Bill Murray start to manipulate his life to work for him instead of struggling to get out of the recurring nightmare?

- ◆ How do you manipulate your life to work for you?

- ◆ What skills would you start practicing right now if you knew you had an eternity to work on them?

- Do you ever feel like you have no effect on the people around you? What can you do differently to try to have an effect on them?

- What limitations would you have if you had to live only one day over and over again?

- What is the greatest good we can do while we are here on Earth?

Leaders

36

Power corrupts, absolute power corrupts absolutely.
—Lord Acton (Bartlett, 1968, p. 750)

Who do young people see as leaders in our society, and what qualities do they see as important for leadership?

- What abilities make a good leader? Who are good leaders of the country? How about your school? Who would you say is a leader among your friends?

- Are you a good leader? Would you want to be a leader? Do you expect more of someone who is considered a leader? What do you expect?

- Are you a good follower? What qualities make a good follower? If your friends want to do something and you don't, what usually happens? Can you think of a specific time when that happened?

- If Hollywood wanted to make a movie about you and your friends going on an adventure, what would the adventure be? What would you be doing? Who would be leading and who would be following?

◆ Essay Prompt

(Expository) Describe the qualities that are important to be a good leader.

◆ Extension Activity

Talk to your principal or some other authority who is in a position of leadership. Ask what qualities he or she believes are needed to be a good leader.

◆ Video

In *War of the Buttons* (Gelin, Nichols, Marsil, & Roberts, 1981), two groups of boys fight over territory in small towns in Great Britain. The movie focuses on the two boys who are the leaders of each group. The boys develop various strategies for battling each other, but in the end both are blamed for the troubles in their villages. The boys end up together in a reformatory.

- ◆ Why do you think Fergus and Geronimo are the leaders of their groups of boys?
- ◆ Have you ever started just playing around and ended up in a fight?
- ◆ Have you ever started out arguing constantly with someone and ended up as a friend?
- ◆ Do adults have arbitrary lines of territory that they fight over?
- ◆ Have you ever been caught in a situation where you had to be friendly to people you didn't like?
- ◆ What were the similarities between the two groups in the movie? What were the differences?
- ◆ How did the boys act like real soldiers?
- ◆ Can you remember a situation where someone put you down and you got back at him or her? How did you feel?

- If you were the leader and one of your group ran into a trap (against your orders), would you try to rescue him or her?

- Have you ever been caught by the teacher when you weren't paying attention in class?

- How important is it for a leader to stick up for his or her followers?

- Why do the buttons take on so much importance?

- Could there be a society where everyone is equal?

- Have you ever made a fort and then defended it against another group?

- Would you rather be defending a castle from the inside or attacking it from the outside?

- What happens to Fergus and Geronimo after they leave the reformatory?

Related Reading ◆

Lord of the Flies (Golding, 1954) is a gripping novel that exposes man's innermost fear, that of returning to his animalistic nature. A group of prep school boys are marooned on a deserted island. One boy tries to keep a measure of order and society while most of the boys follow a second leader into the chaos of instinct. Parts of the book can be disturbing, so it certainly wouldn't be recommended for all classroom situations.

- What kinds of rules do we need as a society? As a school? In a classroom? At home?

- Do we have to have rules to survive?

- Why do we vote for a leader in school? As a country?

- Why do we have age restrictions for voting? Why do we have age restrictions for our national leaders?

- How have qualifications for leaders changed in the past 1,000 years?

- After the boys quit following the system (keeping the fires going), what happened to their society?

- Who makes the rules for our society?

- What qualities does Piggy bring to the society? Do you know anyone like Piggy? How is that person treated?

- What have we gained by moving away from our animal instincts? What have we lost? Do you think people are basically good or bad?

- At the end of the book, Ralph cries for his loss of innocence. What will become of him for the rest of his life? What will happen to Jack?

- Rewrite the end of the story without the rescue.

Lies

37

We lie loudest when we lie to ourselves.

—Eric Hoffer (Peter, 1977, p. 311)

For many students, the line between lies and truths is so thin it is nonexistent.

♦ Quibbling is the art of telling the truth but not quite all of the truth so you mislead someone. For example, your mother asks why you were late and you say your watch stopped, but you don't mention the fact that it stopped 2 weeks ago. Do you ever quibble? Can you imagine yourself quibbling? What would the conversation be like?

♦ The Air Force Academy has an honor code that says that if you see a fellow cadet cheating, you have to turn him or her in. If you don't and the Air Force finds out, you get kicked out of the academy just like the cheater. Do you think that is fair? Would it be a good way to stop cheating? Would you be willing to agree to rules like that in order to do something you really wanted?

♦ Have you ever cheated on a test? How about on an assignment? Do you think it makes any difference if students cheat in school? Why do teachers care so much about students' cheating?

- ◆ President Clinton said he misled people but he didn't lie. Do you think there is a difference? Are there certain people you would not lie to? Are there certain circumstances where you would not lie?

◆ Essay Prompt

(Persuasive) Agree or disagree with the statement, "An honor code (requiring students to turn in cheaters) would be the best way to eliminate cheating in school."

◆ Extension Activity

Try going for a whole day (or a week) telling only the complete truth and see if makes any difference in the way you interact with other people.

◆ Video

Liar, Liar (Grazer & Shadyas, 1997) starts with an excellent concept, a lawyer whose son wishes that his father wouldn't lie. For 24 hours the father (Jim Carey) has to tell the truth, and it almost ruins him. In the end, he learns what is truly important in his life. There are several sexual comments and situations, so be sure to preview the film.

- ◆ Why do many people have such a low opinion of lawyers?

- ◆ Who is the smoothest talker you know?

- ◆ What was the best birthday you can remember?

- ◆ Who is the most insincere person you know?

- ◆ If you were paid to lie, would you do it?

- ◆ Is keeping your word important to you?

- ◆ What is the biggest wish you ever had come true?

- ◆ Why does Jim Carey's wife want to leave him? Why does she want to stick with him?

- ◆ Do your parents ever tell you they will do something and then not follow through? How about your teachers?

- ◆ If you trust someone, does it hurt more when that person doesn't keep his or her word?

- Would you want your parents (or friends) always to be truthful? Are you always truthful with them?

- Do you have any heroes?

- How would you feel if they let you down?

- How could always telling the truth change your life?

Related Reading

Liars (Petersen, 1992) is written at an easy reading level and describes an eighth grader growing up in a small California town. He develops the ability to tell when people are lying, and that ability has a profound effect on his relationships with his father, his friends, and the other townspeople. In a connected subplot, a mystery develops among the major characters in the town.

- Do you believe in ESP?

- Do you think we all have some powers that go beyond our rational natures?

- Would you be afraid to talk to a friend who could tell if you were lying?

- Some people give hints with their body when they are lying. Have you ever been able to tell when someone didn't want to talk to you or when they lied to you?

- Would you want to know every time someone lied to you? Why or why not?

- What kinds of jobs would work best for someone with Sam's ability?

- Can you think of a meal where you were so uncomfortable you couldn't remember what you ate? Do you ever sit down to eat with your parents when you are angry with them?

- How does Sam's relationship with his father change throughout the book?

- How does his relationship to Carmen change?

- Have you ever developed special words like *sot* and *motsot* with your friends?

- Are there things you wish you could talk to your parents about but don't feel comfortable enough to tell them?

Truths

38

When a man comes to me for advice, I find out the kind of advice he wants and I give it to him.

—Josh Billings (Peter, 1977, p. 44)

In order to know what it means to tell the truth, young people must discover what truths they hope to live.

- If a good friend asks you a question and you can either tell the truth and hurt your friend's feelings or lie and make your friend happy, what do you do? Why? What if you are on a date with someone you really like and the same thing happens?

- Someone once asked if I wrote lies in my journal. Do you ever make up stories about yourself? Do you like to tell people about your past experiences? Do you ever exaggerate when you tell them? What is the biggest story you ever told? Do you ever lie to yourself?

- Whom do you trust the most? How do you show that you trust this person? Is there someone to whom you could tell anything about yourself? Do you want to be able to tell your spouse everything? Is it easier to confess things about yourself to a professional (like a psychiatrist), someone you won't ever see again, or to a friend?

♦ Do people confide in you? Have you ever been told something in secret and then been caught telling it to someone else? How did that feel? Have you ever told someone a secret and then found out that person told someone else? How did you feel? What did it do to your relationship with that person?

Essay Prompt

(Narrative) What is the biggest story you have ever told?

Extension Activity

Go to your parents and ask them if they are always truthful with you. Maybe you can make a promise to be truthful to them.

Video

Contact (Zemeckis, 1997) asks the question, Who should represent the Earth if we contact other worlds? Jodie Foster gives it her best try. The movie is science fiction but very philosophical in nature.

♦ Do you believe in intelligent life outside our own?

♦ Do you believe in life after death?

♦ Would you be a good representative of Earth to be sent to other worlds?

♦ Would you want to be sent to other worlds if you weren't sure you would return?

♦ Should someone who represents all of the people of the Earth have spiritual beliefs?

♦ Do you think the super-rich have more influence in our society than the super-intelligent?

♦ Are you interested in astronomy? Would you want to be an astronaut?

♦ Have you ever done something well and had someone else take the credit?

♦ Can science and religious theories coexist?

- On what criteria would you choose one person to represent all the people of Earth?

- Is faith an important part of your life?

- Do you believe the government has hidden secrets of aliens landing on Earth?

- What is the one question you would ask of an intelligent life form that came from a world beyond our own?

Sickness

39

The most important thing in illness is never to lose heart.
—Vladimir Ilyich Lenin (Princeton
Language Institute, 1993, p. 408)

Physical health and sickness is just one of the many issues that every teenager has to deal with.

- Why are doctors so respected in our society? Why are doctor shows so popular on television and in the movies? Why do mothers always seem to want their children to grow up to be doctors? Would you want to be a doctor or go into the field of medicine?

- Have you ever taken care of someone? Do you think you feel better about yourself when you think about others? Is there someone you could help right now, either mentally or physically?

- Do you get sick very often? Do you ever fake being sick to get out of doing something or going somewhere? How do your parents treat you when you are sick? Do you get babied? Do you like to stay in bed all day when you are sick? Have you ever noticed how good you feel after you recover from a sickness?

- Do you get sick more often when you are depressed? How important is your mental state when you get sick? Do you get depressed very often? Describe how you feel when you are depressed. What do you do? Do you know how to get yourself back to feeling better again?

◆ Essay Prompt

(Narration) Tell about the time you felt the sickest.

◆ Extension Activity

Visit a hospital or someone who is sick, and see how you feel afterward.

◆ Video

The Cure (Burg, Eisner, & Horton, 1995) is the story of a young boy with AIDS and his friend who overcomes his fears of the disease. The boys try to make a trip to New Orleans to find a cure. The cure doesn't exist, but their friendship makes the last weeks of a deadly disease bearable for the young boy. The film is as much about friendship and family as it is about sickness.

- ◆ What can you tell about Eric before you ever see his face?
- ◆ Why does Eric throw the rock at the other boys?
- ◆ What do you know about AIDS?
- ◆ Would you be prejudiced against someone who had AIDS?
- ◆ Do your parents call you by a nickname? Are you ashamed of the nickname?
- ◆ How much of prejudice is passed on from parents? How much is passed on through society?
- ◆ Have you been grounded by your parents before? What did you do?
- ◆ Do you read the *National Enquirer* or similar tabloids?
- ◆ If you or your child had an incurable disease, would you be optimistic and try every possible cure, or would you simply accept your fate?

- If you knew you were dying soon, would you try to prolong your life, or would you do the things you always wanted to try even if doing them would shorten your life?

- Have you ever helped a friend through a tough time? How did you feel?

- In what ways did Dexter and Eric help each other?

- What would have happened to Dexter if Eric hadn't been around?

- How do you think Eric will change because of his friendship with Dexter?

Health

40

You are what you eat.
—Anthelme Brillat-Savarin
(Bartlett, 1968, p. 484)

Teenagers are notorious for unhealthy diets, but they also worry about their physical attractiveness.

- Do you usually eat healthy foods or unhealthy foods? What are your typical meals? Do you usually eat by yourself or with other people? Which do you prefer?

- What are your favorite foods? What is your all-time favorite thing to eat? If you could eat one food and only one food for a week, what would you choose?

- Besides food, what other habits do you have that are healthy or unhealthy? Why do you think people in our society are so obsessed with being skinny and exercising?

- Of what part of your body are you most proud? What part would you change if you could? Why? Would you ever get plastic surgery? Why or why not?

Essay Prompt ◆

(Persuasive) Agree or disagree with the statement, "Your mind is just as important to your health as your body."

Extension Activity ◆

Try eating only healthy foods for a week, and see how you feel.

Video ◆

Running Brave (Englander & Everett, 1983) is much more than a sports story. It is the story of Billy Mills, a Native American, who triumphs over tremendous odds to win an Olympic gold medal. Not only does he defeat the world record holder, he overcomes prejudice and the poverty of a reservation childhood. This film could easily be used with the "Equality," "Sports," "Talents," or "Being Alone" sections.

- ◆ What is a stereotype?

- ◆ What stereotypes of Native Americans did the coach have?

- ◆ What stereotypes of Native Americans do you have?

- ◆ How do stereotypes come about?

- ◆ Do you belong to a cultural group that has a stereotype associated with it?

- ◆ How important is winning to you? How much would you sacrifice to win a gold medal at the Olympics? Would you be willing to take illegal drugs in order to win?

- ◆ What evidences of prejudice do you see in the movie?

- ◆ The coach says a man doesn't stand for much unless he wins. Do you agree?

- ◆ Do you think the coach cares more about winning or about Billy?

- ◆ Have you had any coaches like the one in the movie?

- ◆ Do you think Billy's teammates hurt him or help him do better?

- ◆ How is the university better for Billy than the reservation? How is it worse?

- Do you listen when people put you down, or do you try to prove them wrong?

- How do you react when someone disappoints you?

- Why do people cheer so much for U.S. athletes during the Olympics and then pretty much ignore them the rest of the time?

- If you were 24 and had fulfilled your biggest dreams, what would you do with the rest of your life?

- How would you feel if everyone who had put you down was cheering for you?

Personality

41

There are two kinds of people in the world—those who walk into a room and say "There you are" and those who say "Here I am!"

—Abigail Van Buren (Princeton
Language Institute, 1993, p. 332)

Because so much of getting along in society depends on one's personality and intelligence, it's good for students to examine their mental strengths and weaknesses.

◆ Do you enjoy spending time with your friends, or do you tend to spend most of your free time by yourself? At a dance or party, are you someone who hangs back, or are you considered the life of the party? Would you rather have a job working with others or working by yourself? Do you get nervous if you have to talk in front of a crowd, or do you like the attention?

◆ Psychologists divide people into introverts (people who would rather be by themselves or with just a few people) and extroverts (people who would rather be surrounded by lots of other people). Into which category would you put yourself? Why? Would you classify yourself as an optimist (someone who tries to look on the bright side of situations) or a pessimist (someone who plans for the worst). Which outlook do you feel is better? Why?

◆ A man named Howard Gardner came up with seven different intelligences: artistic, mathematical, language, sports (movement), knowing yourself, getting along with others, and musical ability. In which areas do you feel most intelligent? In which areas are you weakest? Why?

◆ Which areas of intelligence do schools emphasize? Why? Which do they leave out? What would a class look like that emphasized your strengths?

◆ Essay Prompt

(Persuasive) Agree or disagree with the statement, "When it comes to career success, your ability to get along with others is more important than your intelligence."

◆ Extension Activity

Take a personality test, and see what it tells you about yourself.

◆ Video

Young Einstein (Ross, Roach, & Serious, 1998) takes a bizarre look at the life of a young (and Australian) Albert Einstein. The movie brings out some interesting scientific principles at the start but degenerates into an odd musical ending. The main premise is how to use nuclear energy to put bubbles into beer, so it may not be appropriate in many settings.

◆ Do you believe that humans should live in harmony with the Earth or that we were meant to dominate the world?

◆ Do you feel like you "fit in" in your present situation?

◆ Which scientific principles are featured in the movie?

◆ Are great inventions created through hard work or by inspiration?

◆ Have you ever met someone who was so smart that you didn't know what he or she was talking about?

◆ Do you believe that there are many geniuses around or very few? Why?

◆ Have you ever done something that you thought was really good and then had it overlooked by your family?

◆ Have you ever tried telling people that time is relative when you are late? How do you think people would react?

Related Reading ◆

Fred Waitzkin (1984) writes about his son, who is a top-notch junior chess champion, in *Searching for Bobby Fischer* (also a movie: Rudin, Horberg, Pollack, & Zaillian, 1993). Waitzken tells about the pressures (both internal and parental) in the tense world of junior chess tournaments. The book is also definitely about family relationships and could easily be used with the "Being Alone" section.

◆ Who was Bobby Fischer, and why would someone be searching for him?

◆ Should parents encourage their child to practice the piano or play chess at an early age even when the child would rather be doing something else?

◆ What is a child prodigy? Would they be more common if more parents encouraged their children to practice at an early age?

◆ What do you think happens to child prodigies when they grow up?

◆ What happened to Josh as he got older?

◆ Why was playing in the park good for Josh?

◆ Why was playing in the park bad for Josh?

◆ Who cared more about winning at the tournaments—the children who were playing or their parents? Why?

◆ How would you feel if your 7-year-old child could beat you at a game like chess?

◆ Why do most people consider the ability to play chess a sign of intelligence?

◆ Why do you think most coaches coach young people?

◆ Would you keep playing a sport or game once you knew you couldn't be the best?

◆ Some young people lose much of their childhoods playing a sport like tennis or gymnastics or chess. Is it worth it if they become champions? Is it worth the effort if they don't?

◆ What does the last sentence of the book tell you about Josh?

42 Mysteries

There is really nothing more to say—except why. But since why is difficult to handle one must take refuge in how.

—Toni Morrison (Princeton Language Institute, 1993, p. 366)

Students are given the chance to look at the major questions in their lives.

♦ Do you like books, movies, or television shows that are mysteries? What is there about a mystery that you like or don't like? What is your favorite or least favorite? Do you like police detective stories where you have to figure out "who done it"? Why?

♦ Do you ask a lot of why questions of your teachers? Are you satisfied with the answers you get? Is it easier for you just to do what you are told, or do you feel that you have to understand the reason you are doing something?

♦ Most of us have some mysteries in our lives—like where did the other brown sock go? What is a mystery in your life to which you would like to find an answer? If there was one question about your future that you could have answered right now, what would you want to know?

◆ Do you ever wonder why you are on Earth? Why is the Earth here? If there was one question that you could ask for all humanity, what would it be?

Essay Prompt

(Poetry) Write a poem that asks "Why?"

Extension Activity

Find out the difference between inductive and deductive reasoning, and see which kind you use most often.

Video

The Fugitive (Koperson & David, 1993) is an action thriller that gets everyone's attention with some major action scenes at the start. Harrison Ford (who plays Dr. Kimball) is sentenced to be executed for the murder of his wife but escapes. He spends the rest of the movie eluding Tommy Lee Jones in order to prove that it was a one-armed man who actually killed his wife.

◆ Have you ever told a story that no one believed? How did that make you feel?

◆ Who is the one person to whom you could tell something and know the person would believe you no matter what you said?

◆ Do some kids tell big stories just so someone will listen to them?

◆ How would the story have been different if Tommy Lee Jones had not believed Harrison Ford? Why does he believe in Dr. Kimball?

◆ Rewrite the second half of the story as though the deputy did not believe the doctor.

◆ Why do the Chicago police doubt the doctor's story?

◆ Would you want a job where you were on call, like a doctor is, if you made lots of money?

◆ Do you enjoy figuring out puzzles?

◆ Would you betray your friend if it could get you out of trouble?

- ◆ Would you help a stranger even if you knew you could get in trouble for helping him or her?

- ◆ How can the news media help or hurt police investigations?

- ◆ Have you ever been betrayed by someone you trusted?

- ◆ Whose job do you think would be more exciting, a U.S. Marshall's or a surgeon's? Which one do you think would be more fulfilling?

- ◆ Have you ever been accused of something you didn't do?

- ◆ Do you know what *vindicated* means?

- ◆ Have you ever felt vindicated?

◆ Related Reading

Sir Arthur Conan Doyle's (1961) *The Hound of the Baskervilles* is a tale of horror set on the moors of England. Sherlock Holmes, by the use of his brilliant mind, is able to uncover the secret of the Baskervilles.

- ◆ Do you know the difference between inductive and deductive reasoning?

- ◆ Which kind of reasoning does Sherlock Holmes use?

- ◆ How important is Dr. Watson to Holmes?

- ◆ Why is Watson important to the author?

- ◆ How does the setting on the moors make the story more mysterious?

- ◆ Do you believe in supernatural creatures like the Loch Ness Monster, Bigfoot, or the Abominable Snowman?

- ◆ How do stories like those get started?

- ◆ What would it take for you to believe or disbelieve those stories?

- ◆ Can you concentrate easily, or are you easily distracted?

- ◆ How much of modern-day police work requires reasoning like Holmes uses?

- ◆ What is the strangest sound you have ever heard?

- ◆ Why do so many horror stories take place at night?

- ◆ Were you ever afraid of the dark?

- ◆ What characteristics do you have that would help you as a detective?

- ◆ Do you think there is a logical explanation for all of our mysteries?

What If...

43

When you get to the end of your rope, tie a knot and hang on.
—Franklin Delano Roosevelt (Princeton
Language Institute, 1993, p. 431)

Many students enjoy dreaming up end-of-the-world scenarios. These scenarios can often be the spark that ignites a creative fire.

- If you were stuck on a deserted island (12 miles across, half jungle, half sand, with plenty of fresh water), what are five things that you would want to have with you? Tell why you would want those five things.

- If you knew there would be a nuclear war in a week, what would you do to prepare? If you were the only one in the United States who knew about the war, who would you tell? Why?

- If you could pick five people who would survive a nuclear war with you, whom would you pick? Why?

- Why do you think people still live near active volcanoes or earthquake fault zones, like the people in and around Los Angeles and San Francisco? Why don't people think much about dying? Do you think they would live differently if they did? Do you think much about dying?

Essay Prompt

(Narrative) Describe what happens to you the day after you have survived a nuclear disaster.

◆ Extension Activity

Research a natural disaster like the eruption of Mt. St. Helens or the San Francisco earthquake to find out what effect it had on the local population.

◆ Video

Deep Impact (Zanuck, Brown, & Leder, 1998) is the story of an asteroid crashing into the Earth. It does a good job of focusing on specific personalities and how they would react to the possible ending of life as we know it. Crude language makes previewing a must.

- Can you joke with your parents over the mistakes they make?

- How do rumors get enlarged and blown out of proportion?

- Do the news media enlarge stories and blow them out of proportion?

- How are our lives manipulated by the news media?

- If you were the president and you knew the world could end soon, would you let everyone know?

- Do you think society would go on as usual once the president made the announcement?

- Would you keep working if you thought the world would end soon? Why?

- How would you feel if you discovered a comet that could end life on our planet?

- How would you feel right before you blasted off in a rocket?

- What would you say to your family if you knew you were going to die?

- If you had to decide which one million people from the United States would survive, what would you use as a criterion?

- Would you include yourself as one of the people to survive? Why?

- Would you choose to die with your family if you found out that none of them would survive? Would you give up your life to save mankind?

- Do you think people would riot and tear things down if they thought the world was about to end?

Spring

44

Earth laughs in flowers.
—Ralph Waldo Emerson (Princeton
Language Institute, 1993, p. 179)

Spring brings with it a great many emotions and associations, especially for young people.

♦ What do you think of when you think of spring? What are the signs of spring? Do you like spring compared to other seasons? What is your favorite season? Why?

♦ Do you think you would appreciate the warmth of spring if it weren't for the coldness of winter? Do you like the changing seasons, or would you rather live where it was sunny and warm all the time? Some people are greatly affected by the increased darkness of winter and the light of spring and summer. Does the change in the amount of sunlight affect you?

♦ Do you think our lives would be better if we didn't have bad times to contrast with the good or sad times to contrast with the happy? What would your life be like if you didn't have any more troubles? Would life get boring?

♦ Some people bounce from really happy to really sad in a matter of moments; other people stay at an even emotional level. Which type are you? Do you wish you were less emotional or more emotional? Why is emotion good or bad?

◆ Essay Prompt

(Expository) Describe a beautiful spring day.

◆ Extension Activity

Go outside on a nice spring day, and lie down in a field. Enjoy the sensations of warmth and new life that come with springtime.

◆ Video

Desert Bloom (Hausman & Corr, 1986) is the story of a teenage girl growing up with an alcoholic stepfather. The film is all about family relationships as the girl grows into a deeper understanding of who she is. It takes place against the backdrop of nuclear testing in Las Vegas during the time when no one knew what effect the testing would have. There isn't much action, and some of the scenes may hit too close to home to be appropriate for all students.

   ◆ Are you a collector of things?
   ◆ Do you have a parent who "has a way of seeing things" or, in other words, tends to overlook all of the bad things because he or she doesn't want to see them?
   ◆ Have you ever gotten new glasses or looked at the world in a completely new way?
   ◆ Where is the safest place in the world for you?
   ◆ What will you remember from this year, as you look back 20 years from now?
   ◆ Do you have a favorite aunt or uncle?
   ◆ What was everyone in the United States afraid of in the early 1950s?
   ◆ How would you feel if you had to wear dog tags?
   ◆ How can one person's problems affect that person's entire family?
   ◆ How can one person's problems affect the entire class?
   ◆ What does Rose mean when she says she was happy he was gone but afraid he wouldn't come back?
   ◆ Why do people stay in dysfunctional relationships?
   ◆ Have you ever forgiven someone who has hurt you badly?
   ◆ How do you think Rose's life will change?

Graduation

45

Its often safer to be in chains than to be free.
—Franz Kafka (Princeton Language
Institute, 1993, p. 185)

Graduation brings out a lot of emotions and gives the students a chance to examine what brings them happiness.

♦ Who is the happiest person you know? If you picked yourself, who is the second happiest? What is it about this person that sets him or her apart as being happy? Someone once said that no matter what happens, it is still a person's choice to be happy or not. Do you think that is true, or is it what happens to us that determines whether we are happy?

♦ Do you focus on your failures or your successes? Are you a perfectionist, or do you just try to get things done? Are you different at school than you are at home? Do you know anyone you consider the opposite of you? Do you get along with that person?

♦ Many people have a big celebration when they graduate from high school even though high school is usually easier than the adult life they will be starting. Do you think they are thinking ahead or looking back? Is graduation just another excuse for a party, or is it something special?

♦ What are your immediate plans and long-term goals after high school? Do you plan to go to your high school reunions? Why or why not? Will you try to stay in touch with your high school friends? Why or why not?

◆ Essay Prompt

(Expository) Describe the happiest person you know.

◆ Extension Activity

Talk to several soon-to-be graduates to find out if they are looking ahead or if they are just glad to be finished with high school.

◆ Video

The movie *With Honors* (Weinstein, Robinson, & Keshishian, 1994) tells the story of a senior at Harvard who learns many lessons about life from a homeless man. They get together because of a senior paper, and the homeless man actually has more to teach about life than the professors at the university. The old man dies, but his lessons stick with the students.

- Have you ever had a major project or test that your entire grade depended on?

- If you were homeless, where would you try to live?

- Would you say most homeless people are worthless human beings, psychologically unstable, or something else? What do you usually do when you see a homeless person?

- Are the homeless victims of their own choices or of other circumstances?

- What food would you ask for if you were homeless and hungry?

- Who was Walt Whitman?

- Where can you learn more—on the street or in the classroom?

- Is experience more important than education?

- When you write, do you rely on your own experience, or do you try to write what you think other people want to hear?

- Do you think your views of life will change as you get closer to dying?

- Could you forgive your father if he had walked out on you when you were a child?

- Will you graduate life with honors and without regret? Why?

References

Books ◆

Angelou, M. (1969). *I know why the caged bird sings.* New York: Bantam.

Armstrong, W. H. (1969). *Sounder.* New York: Scholastic.

Babbitt, N. (1975). *Tuck everlasting.* New York: Farrar, Straus & Giroux.

Bartlett, J. (Ed.). (1968). *Bartlett's familiar quotations* (14th ed.). Boston: Little, Brown.

Creech, S. (1994). *Walk two moons.* New York: HarperCollins.

Cushman, K. (1995). *The midwife's apprentice.* New York: HarperCollins.

Doyle, A. C. (1961). *The hound of the Baskervilles.* New York: Random House.

Golding, W. (1954). *Lord of the flies.* New York: Perigee.

Griffin, J. H. (1960). *Black like me.* New York: Signet.

Haley, A., & Malcolm X. (1964). *The autobiography of Malcolm X.* New York: Ballantine.

Hanson, H. (Ed.). (1948). *O'Henry stories.* New York: Washington Square.

Hedges, P. (1991). *What's eating Gilbert Grape.* New York: Poseidon.

Henry, L. C. (Ed.). (1945). *5,000 quotations for all occasions.* Philadelphia: Blakiston.

Hinton, S. E. (1967). *The outsiders.* New York: Viking.

Johnson, C. (1972). *To see a world in a grain of sand.* Norwalk, CT: Gibson Co.

Kovic, R. (1976). *Born on the Fourth of July.* New York: McGraw-Hill.

Lamb, C., & Lamb, M. (1972). *Tales from Shakespeare*. San Rafael, CA: Leswing Press.

London, J. (1981). *The unabridged Jack London*. Philadelphia: Running Press.

Lowry, L. (1993). *The giver*. New York: Houghton Mifflin.

Paulsen, G. (1987). *Hatchet*. New York: Aladdin.

Paulsen, G. (1994). *The car*. Orlando, FL: Harcourt Brace.

Peter, L. (Ed.). (1977). *Ideas for our time*. New York: William Morrow.

Petersen, P. J. (1992). *Liars*. New York: Simon & Schuster.

Princeton Language Institute. (1993). *21st century dictionary of quotations*. New York: Philip Leif Group.

Sachar, L. (1998). *Holes*. New York: Farrar, Straus & Giroux.

Safir, L., & Safire, W. (1982). *Good advice*. New York: New York Times Books.

Service, R. (1940). *The best of Robert Service*. Toronto: McGraw-Hill Ryerson.

Simpson, J. (1988). *Touching the void*. New York: HarperCollins.

Strunk, W., & White, E. B. (1979). *The elements of style*. New York: Macmillan.

Waitzken, F. (1984). *Searching for Bobby Fischer*. New York: Random House.

Walker, A. (1982). *The color purple*. New York: Harcourt Brace.

Wiesel, E. (1960). *Night*. New York: Bantam.

◆ Videos

Abbott, E., Greenhut, R. (Producers), & Marshall, P. (Director). (1992). *A league of their own* [Film] (126 min.). Hollywood, CA: Columbia Pictures.

Albert, T. (Producer), & Ramis, H. (Director). (1993). *Groundhog day* [Film] (103 min.). Hollywood, CA: Columbia Pictures.

Albert, T. (Producer), & Ramis, H. (Director). (1996). *Multiplicity* [Film] (117 min.). Hollywood, CA: Columbia Pictures.

Arnold, S., Roth, D. (Producers), & Chechik, J. (Director). (1993). *Benny and Joon* [Film] (98 min.). Culver City, CA: MGM Studios.

Avnet, J., Turner, J. (Producers), & Avnet, J. (Director). (1994). *The war* [Film] (125 min.). Universal City, CA: Universal Studios.

Bennett, H. (Producer), & Nimoy, L. (Director). (1986). *Star Trek IV: The voyage home* [Film] (119 min.). Hollywood, CA: Paramount.

Burg, M., Eisner, E. (Producers), & Horton, P. (Director). (1995). *The cure* [Film] (99 min.). Universal City, CA: Universal Studios.

Capra, F. (Producer, Director). (1946). *It's a wonderful life* [Film] (129 min.). Los Angeles: Liberty/Republic Pictures.

Carroll, G. (Producer), & Rosenberg, S. (Director). (1967). *Cool hand Luke* [Film] (126 min.). Burbank, CA: Warner Bros.

Colleton, S., Abbott, E., Greenhut, R. (Producers), & Marshall, P. (Director). (1994). *Renaissance man* [Film] (129 min.). Burbank, CA: Buena Vista.

Cort, R., Nolin, M., Field, T. (Producers), & Herek, S. (Director). (1995). *Mr. Holland's opus* [Film] (142 min.). Los Angeles: Panavision.

Devlin, D. (Producer), & Bill, T. (Director). (1980). *My bodyguard* [Film] (126 min.). Universal City, CA: 20th Century Fox.

Englander, I. (Producer), & Everett, D. (Director). (1983). *Running brave* [Film] (107 min.). Burbank, CA: Buena Vista.

Fied, R., Woods, C. (Producers), & Anspaugh, D. (Director). (1993). *Rudy* [Film] (112 min.). Hollywood, CA: Tristar Pictures.

Finerman, W., Tisch, S., Starkey, S. (Producers), & Zemeckis, R. (Director). (1994). *Forrest Gump* [Film] (142 min.). Hollywood, CA: Paramount.

Foster, D., Truman, L. (Producers), & Hanson, C. (Director). (1994). *The river wild* [Film] (108 min.). Universal City, CA: Universal Studios.

Gelin, X., Nichols, D., Marsil, S. (Producers), & Roberts, J. (Director). (1981). *War of the buttons* [Film] (97 min.). Burbank, CA: Warner Bros.

Gordon, L. (Producer), & Robinson, P. (Director). (1989). *Field of dreams* [Film] (106 min.). Universal City, CA: Universal Studios.

Gottlieb, L., Bergstein, E. (Producers), & Ardolino, E. (Director). (1987). *Dirty dancing* [Film] (97 min.). Van Nuys, CA: Vestron Pictures.

Grazer, B. (Producer), & Howard, R. (Director). (1989). *Parenthood* [Film] (124 min.). Universal City, CA: Universal Studios.

Grazer, B. (Producer), & Lynn, J. (Director). (1994). *Greedy* [Film] (113 min.). Los Angeles: Imagine Entertainment.

Grazer, B. (Producer), & Shadyas, T. (Director). (1997). *Liar, liar* [Film] (97 min.). Universal City, CA: Universal Studios.

Grazer, B. (Producer), & Zieff, H. (Director). (1992). *My girl* [Film] (102 min.). Hollywood, CA: Columbia Pictures.

Haft, S., Witt, P., Thomas, T. (Producers), & Weir, P. (Director). (1989). *Dead poets society* [Film] (128 min.). Burbank, CA: Buena Vista.

Hausman, M. (Producer), & Corr, E. (Director). (1986). *Desert bloom* [Film] (106 min.). Hollywood, CA: Paramount.

Jacobs, A. (Producer), & Schaffner, F. (Director). (1968). *Planet of the apes* [Film] (112 min.). Universal City, CA: 20th Century Fox.

Jaffe, S., Lansing, S. (Producers), & Mandel, R. (Director). (1992). *School ties* [Film] (110 min.). Hollywood, CA: Paramount.

Koperson, A. (Producer), & David, A. (Director). (1993). *The fugitive* [Film] (127 min.). Burbank, CA: Warner Bros.

Musca, T. (Producer), & Menendez, R. (Director). (1987). *Stand and deliver* [Film] (103 min.). Burbank, CA: Warner Studios.

Powell, M. (Producer), & Kleiser, R. (Director). (1991). *White fang* [Film] (109 min.). Burbank, CA: Walt Disney Studios.

Richmil, M., Melnick, D. (Producers), & Schepisi, F. (Director). (1987). *Roxanne* [Film] (107 min.). Hollywood, CA: Columbia Pictures.

Roos, F., Fredrickson, G. (Producers), & Coppola, F. (Director). (1983). *The outsiders* [Film] (91 min.). Hollywood, CA: Zoetrope Studios.

Ross, W., Roach, D., Serious, Y. (Producers), & Serious, Y. (Director). (1998). *Young Einstein* [Film] (90 min.). Burbank, CA: Warner Bros.

Rudin, S., Horberg, W., Pollack, S. (Producers), & Zaillian, S. (Director). (1993). *Searching for Bobby Fischer* [Film] (110 min.). Hollywood, CA: Paramount.

Rudin, S. (Producer), & Weir, P. (Director). (1998). *The Truman show* [Film] (103 min.). Hollywood, CA: Paramount.

Saxon, E. (Producer), & Demme, J. (Director). (1993). *Philadelphia* [Film] (122 min.). Hollywood, CA: Tristar Pictures.

Schwartz, R., Palmer, P. (Producers), & Haid, C. (Director). (1994). *Iron Will* [Film] (109 min.). Burbank, CA: Walt Disney Studios.

Shuler, L. (Producer), & Donner, R. (Director). (1985). *Ladyhawke* [Film] (121 min.). Burbank, CA: Warner Bros.

Simon, S., Bain, B. (Producers), & Ward, V. (Director). (1998). *What dreams may come* [Film] (114 min.). Beverley Hills, CA: PolyGram Pictures.

Spielberg, S. (Producer, Director). (1985). *The color purple* [Film] (152 min.). Burbank, CA: Warner Bros.

Teper, M., Ohlsson, B., Matalon, D. (Producers), & Hallstrom, L. (Director). (1994). *What's eating Gilbert Grape* [Film] (117 min.). Hollywood, CA: Paramount.

Weinstein, P., Robinson, A. (Producers), & Keshishian, A. (Director). (1994). *With honors* [Film] (103 min.). Burbank, CA: Warner Bros.

Worth, M. (Producer), & Lee, S. (Director). (1992). *Malcolm X* [Film] (201 min.). Burbank, CA: Warner Bros.

Yates, P. (Producer, Director). (1979). *Breaking away* [Film] (100 min.). Universal City, CA: 20th Century Fox.

Zanuck R., Brown, D. (Producers), & Howard, R. (Director). (1985). *Cocoon* [Film] (117 min.). Universal City, CA: 20th Century Fox.

Zanuck, R., Brown, D. (Producers), & Leder, M. (Director). (1998). *Deep impact* [Film] (121 min.). Hollywood, CA: Paramount.

Zemeckis, R. (Producer, Director). (1997). *Contact* [Film] (150 min.). Burbank, CA: Warner Bros.